D0769741

COUNTRY LIVING
AMERICAN
GLASSWARE

what is it? | what is it worth?

Joe L. Rosson

Helaine Fendelman

House of Collectibles

New York   Toronto   London   Sydney   Auckland

House of Collectibles and colophon are registered trademarks of Random House, Inc.

RANDOM HOUSE is a registered trademark of Random House, Inc.

Country Living is a trademark of Hearst Communications, Inc.

This book is available at special discounts for bulk purchases for sales promotions or premiums. Special editions, including personalized covers, excerpts of existing books, and corporate imprints, can be created in large quantities for special needs. For more information, write to Random House, Inc., Special Markets/ Premium Sales, 1745 Broadway, MD 6-2, New York, NY, 10019 or e-mail *specialmarkets@randomhouse.com*.

Please address inquiries about electronic licensing of any products for use on a network, in software, or on CD-ROM to the Subsidiary Rights Department, Random House Information Group, FAX 212-572-6003.

Visit the House of Collectibles Web site: www.houseofcollectibles.com

Library of Congress Cataloging-in-Publication Data is available.

First Edition

0 9 8 7 6 5 4 3 2 1

ISBN-10: 0-375-72117-7

ISBN-13: 978-0-375-72117-5

Printed in China

748.20973
ROSS

Contents

PRESSED GLASS

Acknowledgments

W e have been overwhelmed by the generosity of the people who have helped us.

Our first thank you goes to Dorothy Harris, and to Jackie Deval at Country Living Books, for believing in this project as much as we do.

We particularly want to thank the staff and owners of Green Valley Auctions, located between Washington, D. C., and Richmond, V.A. They supplied us with wonderful photographs and a great deal of information, and we want to thank Jeffrey S. Evans for making this possible. Special thanks also go to Karen Reed, head of the Catalog Department, and Dustin Kline, Internet technology director. Karen has an especially warm place in our hearts because she supplied much helpful information.

Thanks to Rebecca J. Davis at Northeast Auctions in Portsmouth, N.H. and Lynda Cain at Samuel T. Freeman & Company in Philadelphia, P.A., who always said "yes" to whatever photographs were requested.

A big thank you is appropriate for Chattanooga, TN's Houston Museum for allowing us full access to their wonderful collection. Special thanks go to the director of the Houston Museum, Amy Frierson, for her kindness.

We also want to thank Chris Paddleford of Kingston Pike Antiques Mall and Linda Dodd of the Farragut Antiques Mall, both in Knoxville, TN, for their willingness to help. Our appreciation goes to William H. McGuffin, who took the photographs from Green Valley, and Richard H. Crane, who took the rest of the photographs and generously supplied his computer savvy to make this project work. For complete photo credits please see page 202.

Introduction

When people think about the objects that are valuable in their houses, they mainly think of the furniture, the silver, and perhaps the artwork. They seldom think of glass.

A few years ago, we were called in to evaluate the household contents of a lady who found herself in need of money and had to liquidate some of her personal property. She hoped that we would find a treasure worth a great deal of money and eagerly showed us her furniture, which was not antique; her grandmother's silver, which was silver plated; and her "Currier and Ives" prints, which were all reproductions.

As we were leaving our somewhat disheartened client, we happened to notice a glass vase filled with brown wilted flowers that was sitting among other vases and flower pots on a rickety shelf out in the garage. The vase was a cylinder about 10 inches tall and was made from blue glass that had a lovely iridescent finish (at least it did after we got all the dust and dirt off the surface). The vase was decorated with columns of roses that terminated in leaves at the top. Removing the flowers with great speed—but with much care—we found that the vase was a circa 1910 carnival glass vase made by the short-lived Millersburg Glass of Millersburg, Ohio. It was in a pattern called "Rose Column" and, in blue, a very rare piece.

Checking it over, we found that the vase was in very good condition with no chips, cracks, scratches, or discolorations. Our client did not understand why we were so excited about a glass vase that she just used to hold the occasional bouquet of posies cut from her garden, but we explained to her that this was the one piece in her home that was worth a substantial amount of money.

Many people do not understand the value that a piece of glass might have. Sometimes small, outwardly unassuming pieces can have a considerable monetary worth, and our client was surprised when her carnival glass vase sold at auction for $4,500. In this book, we will examine the spectrum of American glass and explore a range of the kinds of glass objects that can be quite valuable, and those that have a more modest monetary worth, and how to tell the difference between the two.

Many collectors tend to include ceramic items (pottery and porcelain) in the same classification as glass, but this simply is not correct because glass is a very specific substance with its own peculiar composition. Glass is made by combining a silicate (some sort of sand, such as silicon dioxide, boric oxide, or aluminum oxide) with an alkali (often potash or soda) and heating it until it becomes a plastic molten mass that can be blown using puffs of air or injected by one of a number of methods into some sort of mold.

Glass is noncrystalline and, scientifically, it is considered to be a super-cooled liquid rather than a solid. It can be transparent, translucent, or opaque, and it can take on a variety of colors depending on the trace elements that are included in the formula for a particular batch. Cobalt, for example, produces glass with a pleasing deep blue tint, while gold produces a "gold-ruby," and a bit of selenium turns glass red.

Glass can be produced naturally by a volcanic eruption, or not so naturally by a nuclear explosion over sandy soil. It is thought that man first made glass in Mesopotamia around 3500 BC as a coating for stone or ceramic items, but it was another thousand or so years before objects were made entirely out of glass. Archaeologists have found glass vessels that date to circa 1500 BC around the site of the ancient city of Nineveh, and it is at about that time that Egyptian Pharaoh Tuthmosis III is said to have started a glass industry in Egypt using workers drawn from the Mesopotamian region.

The history of glass making over the next three millennia is long and involved, with important centers of production springing up in such diverse places as Syria, Cyprus, Rhodes, Rome, Venice, and Bohemia, just to name a few. In this book, however, the examination of the development of the glass makers' art around the world will not be our objective. Instead, we will focus on glass made or commonly found in the United States.

The primary focus will be on American-made objects of the nineteenth and twentieth centuries, but a few European-made items will be included either because it is hard to differentiate between similar European and American examples or because the type of glass is widely available in the United States and is an integral part of collecting glass in this country. A good example of this might be "Mary Gregory" glass, which is widely associated with the American Boston and Sandwich Glass Company. However, the vast majority of this ware was made in Europe, with most being produced in Bohemia, which is part of the present-day Czech Republic.

The pieces being discussed will be divided into two specific categories: 1) blown and mold blown glass and 2) pressed glass. Both of these categories encompass a wide variety of objects. Within the blown and mold blown grouping, there will be objects made in the early nineteenth century, but there will also be late nineteenth- and early twentieth-century art glass pieces as well as cut glass from the American Brilliant Period of the late nineteenth and early twentieth centuries.

The pressed glass category will be just as broad, and we will examine the early American pressed glass made in the second quarter of the nineteenth century as well as the pattern glass that was very popular during the last quarter of the nineteenth century and into the first quarter of the twentieth century. The pressed glass category will also include such items as carnival glass and Depression glass.

Within these groupings, we will be showing a variety of examples and discussing their history, manufacturer (if known), identifying characteristics, and values (i.e., what a specific object is and what it is worth). We will also discuss reproductions in the field when that is applicable and how to distinguish the old from the new.

As for what an item is worth, it must be understood that antiques and collectibles have more than one price or value. Among others, there is the price for which items can be sold and there is a somewhat higher price at which the same items should be insured. The latter is called the "insurance replacement value," and it can be defined as the amount of money it would take to replace an item if it were lost, stolen, or destroyed.

This is what it would cost for an owner to go out, find a comparable replacement item, and purchase it from a retail source in an appropriate marketplace, within a reasonable amount of time. In other words, this is a retail value, and these sums are not the amount that private individuals can normally expect to receive for similar objects if they decided to sell.

Sellers can expect to receive what is called "fair market value." This is defined by the Internal Revenue Service as "the price that property would sell for on the open market between a willing buyer and a willing seller, with neither being required to act, and both having reasonable knowledge of the relevant facts." Fair market value is the amount of money that a private individual can usually expect to receive when selling an object; that amount can be thought of as being "wholesale." As a general rule, the "fair market value" is 30 to 60 percent less than the "insurance replacement value."

In these pages, we will be using the "insurance replacement value" standard unless it is otherwise clearly stated that a price was derived from an auction source. These prices taken from auctions are the actual prices including all fees paid for specific pieces. At one time, auction prices were considered to be "fair market value," but over the past few decades, that concept has changed as auctions have increasingly become outlets for very rare items that sell for values closer to or even above retail.

Therefore, auction prices can be open to some interpretation and might be "fair market" or "retail" value. It depends on the circumstances at the auctions, the mood of the bidders, and most important, on the rarity and condition of the piece being sold. Most of the auction prices used here are for rare items with values that are closer to "insurance replacement value" than they are to "fair market value."

We will begin our look into American glass by exploring the beginnings of American glass making in the seventeenth and eighteenth centuries, but we will be showing only one example of the items made during this infancy period because these pieces are very seldom encountered. The average collector rarely sees these examples except in a museum or at a very high-end auction where the pieces will be identified by curators and specialists. There are far too few of these pieces available in the current marketplace to make an in-depth discussion of them meaningful for most of today's collectors, and there are too few of these items being sold to provide a basis for reliable pricing. However, a brief discussion of the roots of nineteenth- and twentieth-century American glass is fundamental to understanding the totality of this subject.

The Birth of American Glass

One of the first manufacturing facilities in America was a glass house in Jamestown, Virginia, and it was established in 1608, just one year after the colony was founded. Jamestown seemed to be a perfect place for this sort of enterprise because there was an abundance of wood in the surrounding forests that provided the necessary fuel to keep the furnaces going.

The idea was to ship finished glass back to England, but this early enterprise failed because of the severe winter of late 1609 to early 1610. A dozen or so years later, in 1621, another factory was started in Jamestown, this one by Venetians who wanted to compete with the English glass makers for whom they had formerly worked. Unfortunately, they too went out of business very quickly, and their last year of operation was 1624.

During the seventeenth and early eighteenth centuries, several other glass houses were founded in the American colonies, but all failed because of labor and technical problems and because American buyers tended to prefer European products. It should be pointed out that the colonies on this side of the Atlantic were set up to be producers of raw material and consumers of English finished goods; the government in London did not want manufacturing of any kind to flourish on these New World shores.

Wistar or 'Wistarberg'

The first successful glass house in the American colonies was started in 1739 by Casper Wistar, a German from Baden. It is said that Wistar arrived in Philadelphia in 1717 with nine cents in his pocket and a double-barreled gun. His first jobs consisted of doing a variety of menial tasks such as hauling ashes for a candle and soap maker, and his first meal in the New World is said to have been all the apples he could eat.

Wistar saved his money and began buying cheap land that he subdivided and resold to fellow German immigrants. Next, he expanded to iron making, which eventually led him to establish a brass button factory in Philadelphia. By the late 1720s, Wistar was so prosperous that he sent to Germany for his brother John, and when he arrived in Philadelphia, Casper set him up in the wine business.

The realities of the wine business pointed out the need for a source of cheap bottles, and Casper Wistar became interested in making glass. In the late 1730s, Wistar began buying land around Alloway Creek in New Jersey and started searching for seasoned glass makers in Germany to bring to America to serve as workers in his glass house.

The land Wistar chose was perfect for his proposed business. It had a good grade of sand, an abundance of wood for fuel, and clay that could be used to make the pots that would hold the molten glass. It was also on a waterway that emptied into the Delaware River, which gave Wistar easy access to prosperous urban markets such as Philadelphia.

The four glass makers Wistar chose drove a hard bargain for their services, and, in fact, Wistar had to make them partners in the enterprise before they would cross the Atlantic to work with him. Wistar had to pay their passage and provide food and servants plus one-third of the profits of the new glass works. In return, the four German glass makers agreed to teach Casper and his son, Richard, the art and science of making glass.

The furnaces for Wistar's glass house were built in 1739, and although most collectors call this company just "Wistar" or "Wistarberg" glass, the company was actually named the "United Glass Company." The company reportedly made three kinds of glass: a watery green glass used for windows, an olive-amber for bottles, and a clear colorless (or "white") glass for decorative or luxury items. There is very little record, however, that there was much white glass made at the United Glass Company, and the shards found on the site are almost always green or olive-brown.

Casper Wistar died in 1752, which was just past his fifty-sixth birthday, and his son Richard took over the family business. Richard continued to make a success of the business until the Revolutionary War. At this point, the history of Wistarberg glass becomes rather cloudy. Evidently, Richard Wistar was a Tory (an English sympathizer), and as the conflict between the fledgling United States and the British empire drew to a close, it is said that Richard Wistar was attacked by a mob in Philadelphia, rescued by General Clinton's retreating army, and taken to Rahway, New Jersey, where he died from his injuries.

That would have been in 1778, but Richard Wistar is known to have died in 1781, so at least part of this legend is not true. It is true that Richard died in Rahway, possibly as a result of his injuries, just a little bit later. In any event, Wistar's glass factory was no longer operating, and it was offered for sale in October 1780.

At this point, it is important to emphasize that there is a significant number of glass articles ascribed to Wistar's operation, but there is no historic or archaeological proof that any of these items were actually made in the Wistar operation. In other words, no one knows with any certainty exactly what an entire piece of Wistar glass actually looks like, and all collectors have is speculation, guess work, and possibilities.

Stiegel

On August 31, 1750, the ship *Nancy* arrived in the port of Philadelphia carrying human cargo of 270 immigrants; among them was Henry William Stiegel, who was born May 13, 1729. Many of the particulars of Stiegel's life are shrouded in the fog of fulsome legend, and tradition has it that he was born in Mannheim, Germany, and was a titular baron, but neither "fact" holds up to close scrutiny. There is some thought that the title "Baron" was conferred on Stiegel by his Mennonite neighbors, who thought that such a grand and flamboyant individual should be a "Baron" at the very least.

Within two years, Stiegel had settled in Lancaster County, Pennsylvania, and married the daughter of Jacob Huber, a prominent local ironmaster who owned one of the oldest iron furnaces in the area. By 1756, Stiegel, along with a Philadelphia partnership, was operating the Huber furnaces, and glass making appears to have begun at the Elizabeth Furnace sometime in 1763 (probably in September). What was actually made here is open to speculation, but it was probably bottles and window glass for the most part.

In 1765, Stiegel started another glass house at Mannheim, Pennsylvania. He established yet another glass house in Mannheim in 1769, which was named the "American Flint Glass Works." Stiegel employed experienced English and German glass workers, and it is said that they turned out a product that was comparable to the glass products made in Germany or England. It is very difficult to separate the products made by Stiegel at Mannheim from their European counterparts of the day.

The glass made at the Mannheim facility was soda-lime glass, flint (or lead) glass, or colored glass that was mainly amethyst, blue, amber, or emerald green. Some pieces were decorated with enamel in the German manner, while others were decorated with wheel engraving in the English style.

Many of the Mannheim products were formed by blowing the glass into a mold that imparted designs, including diamond quilting and a daisy-in-a-square pattern that looks exactly the way it sounds.

Stiegel received a financial boost in 1767 when the Townsend Act levied duties on imported goods and colonial merchants signed agreements of nonimportation saying that they would buy and sell only those goods that were made in America. British goods were soon in short supply, and companies such as Stiegel's prospered with the increased sales.

This was when Stiegel tried to imitate English fancy table wares and introduced a line of wheel-engraved flint glass objects such as decanters and wine glasses. Unfortunately, as a result of poor management and the expense of the production of these luxury wares, the glass house closed in 1774 and Stiegel found himself in debtors' prison.

Amelung

After the Revolutionary War, the new United States government wanted to promote home industry and began searching for individuals who would come to America to set up manufacturing facilities. One of the individuals to answer this call was John Frederick Amelung, who was working at the time as the superintendent of a mirror glass factory in Germany.

The British tried to prevent Amelung from coming to the United States, but he persevered and arrived in Baltimore, Maryland, in 1784. In August of that year, Amelung bought an existing glass house in western Maryland and, within a short period of time, expanded it to four glass houses, which were collectively referred to as "New Bremen" or the "New Bremen Glass Manufactory."

The name was probably derived from the Bremen, Germany, merchants who had financed Amelung's enterprise. Sadly, Amelung was in trouble within three years of starting his glass houses. He complained that sales were poor because Americans still preferred to buy European products (a situation that would plague some American industries until after the Civil War) and that government—be it state or federal—failed to nurture native businesses with tax breaks and/or loans.

Amelung tried to impress his customers and influential governmental officials by making elaborate presentation pieces that were richly engraved. The idea was to show that his products were the equal of any made in Europe, but despite Amelung's efforts, the New Bremen Glass Manufactory failed in 1795.

Although "New Bremen" made bottles and window glass like the other American glass makers working in the 1700s, it is the only eighteenth-century American glass in which signed and dated pieces are known to exist. The known signature is "New Bremen Glasmanufactory" (spelled as one word with one or two "S's" in "Glassmanufactory"). The date may be just the year or, as in the case of the covered tumbler made for Charles Ghequiere of Baltimore, have a more specific notation of time of manufacture—"the 20the of June, 1788."

Despite its early setbacks, the glass making industry in America refused to die. When an important factory such as Wistar, Stiegel, or Amelung closed down, the glass workers just scattered and began to practice their trade in another location. Unfortunately for modern collectors, many of these facilities were small and their products are now impossible to identify with any certainty.

The American glass industry profited from the turmoil in Europe during the first two decades of the nineteenth century. The Napoleonic Wars, the Embargo Act of 1807, which was designed to curtail all English and French exports to the United States, and the subsequent War of 1812 gave a significant boost to the struggling glass industry. During this period alone, more than forty glass houses were in operation in America.

The Tariff of 1824, which placed a duty on imported European glass, helped even further, and by the 1840s, the number of glass houses had almost doubled, to more than eighty. Most of these establishments were in the business of making window glass, liquor bottles, ink bottles, medicine bottles, and other commercially useful pieces of glass. There were, however, a number of companies that made fine tableware from clear, colorless flint glass, and some of the firms making bottles and windowpanes also made lesser quality tableware from the aqua or amber glass that they used in these more utilitarian products. However, it would not be until the invention and perfection of the pressed glass process that the American glass industry would become an important player on the world stage.

BLOWN AND BLOWN MOLDED GLASS

item 1

Stiegel bottle

Valued at $6,780

Bottle, 5¼ inches tall, 3¾ inches greatest
width with a flattened ovoid body and
cylindrical neck. The glass is a
transparent violet color with a design
that consists of diamonds and flowers.
There is a rough pontil that is pushed up
into the base, and the condition is good
except for two small scratches and some
slight surface wear.

what is it? When it was made, a bottle such as this one was designed to serve the most prosaic of purposes. Some early sources refer to bottles like this as being "perfume" flasks, but today, they are most often called "pocket bottles" and were probably designed to hold distilled spirits—although it is documented that one such bottle was used to hold a mixture of camphor and lavender water.

These decorative pocket bottles have their origins in continental Europe, but the pattern on the one pictured above suggests that it was made in the glass works owned by Henry William Stiegel, which was located in Manheim, Pennsylvania, from 1763 to 1774. This particular bottle was blown in mold and is in a pattern that is called the "Diamond-Daisy" design.

Stiegel made these bottles in several patterns. It is speculated that Stiegel made the various molds that were necessary to produce these patterns in his own iron works. Interestingly, it is the plain pocket bottles with no pattern whatsoever that are considered to be extremely rare, along with the examples in the "Hexagon-Daisy" pattern.

It is thought that there is no European equivalent to the "Diamond-Daisy" pattern found on this pocket bottle. This specimen was blown into a mold using one gather of glass, while many of its European counterparts were made using the half-post method, which used two gathers of glass that are clearly visible to the eye in the finished vessel because the bottom of the piece is thicker than the top and there is a line of demarcation. However, it should be stressed that some American flasks were made using this half-post method (in this case, the word "post" refers to a gather of glass).

Stiegel pocket bottles were made in several colors. Most are found in shades of amethyst that range from light to dark, but blue is known as well as clear colorless. Amethyst is considered to be the most common while blue and clear colorless are quite uncommon. This pocket bottle should be dated between 1770 and 1774.

what is it worth? At auction, this piece recently sold for $6,780.

item 2

sunburst flask

what is it? A number of American glass houses made blown-in-mold pieces that had a design that collectors refer to as a "sunburst." There is a great variety to these closely related pieces, and collectors find themselves paying careful attention to the minute details of the design in order to ascertain who the maker might have been.

The example pictured above is very distinctive because it has 24 rays arranged in an oval around what is called a "five-petalled" flower (actually, there are four petals surrounding a central "petal"). Other similar flasks have different numbers of rays arranged around a varying type of center (sometimes these variations can be very subtle), and a variety of treatments on the sides.

Flasks such as this are often identified by a designation originated by George S. and Helen McKearin in their important book, *American Glass*. The example pictured above is known as "GVIII-

Valued at $4,125

5¾-inch-tall flask, in transparent deep puce colored glass. It is a half-pint size and has a cylindrical neck, ribbed sides, a plain lip, and a rough pontil scar. It is decorated with a design that resembles a sunburst. The condition is excellent except for a tiny impact or "bruise" on the edge of the base.

25," which means that this is the twenty-fifth flask in group VIII, which is a category devoted entirely to flasks in the sunburst pattern.

This particular flask is now attributed to the Baltimore Glass Works, which was located in Baltimore, Maryland. There is some disagreement about when this factory was founded, but it was sometime between 1790 and 1799, with a later date being the most likely. It was located on Federal Hill in Baltimore, and several of the glass workers from William Henry Stiegel's defunct glass works are said to have found employment there.

what is it worth? At auction, this flask sold for $4,125.

item3

Washington and Jackson flask

Valued at $750

Bottle, half-pint size, that is 4 inches tall. The glass is yellowish amber with a slight olive tone, and the bottom has a rough pontil. On one side, there is an embossed bust in profile facing right labeled "Washington," and on the other side, there is an embossed bust facing left labeled "Jackson." The piece is in excellent condition with an interior open bubble and some residue.

what is it? Despite our thoughts that our sainted ancestors were either moderate imbibers or teetotalers, the large number of glass whiskey flasks that exist today proves otherwise. This group is called "historical portrait flasks," and these had images of such personages as George Washington, Benjamin Franklin, Zachary Taylor, John Adams, Henry Clay, Dewitt Clinton, General Lafayette, and Andrew Jackson, among others.

It is unclear who made the first of these flasks, but it has been speculated that it may have been the Pitkin Glass Works, which was located in East Manchester, Connecticut, from about 1783 to 1830. Whoever it may have been that made the first historical portrait flask, by 1820, any number of companies were making them, including the Kensington Glass Works in Philadelphia, Knox and McKee in Wheeling, Virginia (now Wheeling, West Virginia), the Baltimore Glass Works of Baltimore, Maryland, and John Robinson of Pittsburgh, Pennsylvania.

The bottle pictured above is known as GI-34 Washington and Jackson portrait flask. It was made by the Coventry Glass Works in Coventry, Connecticut, sometime in the late second or early third quarter of the nineteenth century (i.e., circa 1850), and in this color, it is considered to be a fairly common flask. Flasks such as this are judged by how rare they are, the color of glass, the condition, and how sharp and well defined the impression from the mold happens to be.

Flasks with this design are commonly found in a yellowish amber or a dark olive green. Any other color would be very unusual and would raise the value significantly. The impression from the mold on this piece is good, and the condition is very good.

what is it worth? $750

item4

Pittsburgh sugar bowl

Valued at $2,200

Covered sugar bowl, free blown with pontil on both base and finial. The glass is transparent cobalt blue, and the piece is 7 inches tall with a 3⅞-inch diameter at the rim of the bowl. The bowl is bulbous and has a plain galleried rim, and the foot is rather heavy and was applied separately. The lid is domed with a rim that is folded inward and has a solid tab finial that resembles a button. The piece is in perfect condition.

what is it? Sugar bowls seem so commonplace to us, but to late eighteenth- and early nineteenth-century Americans, a glass sugar bowl was a luxury and a prized possession. It should be mentioned that sugar was a very expensive commodity that people kept under lock and key, and to display it in a beautiful covered bowl was a sign of status and wealth.

After the end of the Revolutionary War, Americans (including many ex-soldiers) began moving westward into what was called the "Midwest." This was basically the land south of Lake Erie to the valley of the Ohio River. This territory included western Pennsylvania (particularly the area around Pittsburgh), Ohio, Kentucky (especially northern Kentucky), Michigan, and what eventually became West Virginia.

Into this area came farmers, merchants, and craftsmen, including skilled glass makers from such places as New Jersey, New Hampshire, New York, and Maryland. For the most part, these glass workers concentrated on meeting the needs of the frontier inhabitants by making bottles and window glass, but they also made the pitchers, bowls, jars, and tumblers that were needed by the more prosperous households for everyday life.

The glassware made in the Midwest was often rather plain with ribs, swirling ribs, diamonds, or no embellishment at all except perhaps applied handles or finials. The sugar bowls made in this region often have a distinctive appearance with a high domed lid that can be bell-shaped and surmounted by a round or flattened round (button-like) finial. Sometimes these lids can have a double dome with a large dome on the bottom surmounted by a smaller dome with a rounded finial on top of that.

This lid is seated on the top of the bowl with a collar-like gallery that can rise up like a parapet around a turret. These sugar bowls can be found in a variety of colors, such as clear colorless, various shades of amber that range from an orange amber to a more yellow amber, various shades of blue including sapphire, cobalt, and aquamarine, green bottle glass, and, very rarely, amethyst that can range from a light shade to almost purple.

This particular sugar bowl is attributed to Pittsburgh, which not only covers that city proper but also part of the region around the city and on the Monongahela River. The first glass house in Pittsburgh was established in 1796 by Gen. James O'Hara and Maj. Isaac Craig, and in 1808, Englishmen Thomas Bakewell and Benjamin Page established a flint glass factory, which is considered to be the first entirely successful flint glass manufacturer in the United States.

Ascribing this piece to a specific factory is impossible, but it was probably made sometime in the first quarter or early in the second quarter of the nineteenth century.

what is it worth?
Sugar bowls are rather difficult to find, and when they are found, they are prized. This one is a particularly attractive cobalt blue and sold at auction for $2,200.

item 5
witch ball

Valued at $605
4½-inch-diameter sphere of
cranberry-colored glass decorated with
white loopings. There is a rough pontil
mark and a small opening at the top.
It is in perfect condition.

what is it?

To modern eyes, this looks like a Christmas tree ornament, and in a way it is the ancestor of those cherished yuletide decorations.

To our ancestors, however, this is a "witch ball," and it was used to ward off evil from the home. There are a number of legends that surround these spheres of glass, and it is a little difficult to say when they were first made and what their actual use might have been.

Some say witch balls originated in Europe during medieval times while others try to stretch the history back to Roman times, but most witch balls date to no earlier than the beginning of the eighteenth century. Typically, a witch ball is a hollow sphere with a diameter from $3\frac{1}{2}$ to $7\frac{1}{2}$ inches, made from blue, red, or green glass. Many were silvered on the inside, but others had marvered loops or spatters of color. Much more modern witch balls have the spatters of color plus strands of glass that run across the interior. The idea was to place these balls in the home near windows or to suspend them near the corner of a ceiling. In addition, they sometimes were placed near the opening of a fireplace. These sparkling glass balls were thought to mesmerize witches or other evil spirits and capture their wicked spells before they could harm the family inside the house.

Some say the evil is caught by the strands inside the ball, and others say that when the homemaker dusted the ball, she removed all the residual evil and banished it from the family's abode. The silvered variety of witch balls were said to reflect the evil or the "evil eye" back to the sender or that any demon that saw its distorted reflection in the curved silvered surface of the ball would flee in fright.

There is yet another story that maintains that glass blowers used witch balls over their annealing ovens. In days gone by, glass blowers put their finished wares in the annealing oven and went home for the night while their glass cooled at a uniform rate. Sometimes, the ovens would malfunction and when the glass maker returned, he would find ruin and disaster and that his labor had been for naught. These calamities were blamed on witches, and witch balls were placed over the ovens to catch the malevolent spells and prevent this mishap.

It is said witch balls evolved into our modern-day glass Christmas ornaments. It is believed that the reflective gold balls were meant symbolically to summon the return of the sun in spring while the silver reflective balls were there to represent the moon and to petition the moon goddess for protection in the approaching new year.

Witch balls should not be confused with spherical net floats that are used by fishermen around the world (particularly in Portugal and Japan). Net floats usually are bottle glass colors (green or brown), and they often have a flattened blob of glass on the end to seal up the opening. True witch balls are generally made from relatively high-quality glass, while net floats are made from bubbly poor-quality glass.

Witch balls were widely made in the United States and Great Britain. The one pictured is thought to be American and was probably made in New England during the third quarter of the nineteenth century.

what is it worth? This witch ball sold at auction in 2005 for $605.

Related Item

Bowl with spherical cover. 6¾-inch-tall globular bowl with a hollow sphere for a cover. The sphere is 3 inches in diameter and rests on the bowl's flared rim. There is a plain circular foot, and the bowl is made from bottle-green transparent glass, while the sphere has a slightly lighter bluish shade. Both pieces are unsigned and undamaged.

What is it?
On rare occasions, it is possible to find a witch ball with a matching stand or holder, but the sphere on top of this sugar bowl is really a lid. Spherical lids can be found on a variety of early American blown-glass pieces, including jugs, jars, and bowls.

These are closely related to witch balls, but they do not seem to have served the same function of preventing evil from entering the house. Instead, they were utilitarian lids that were probably easier for the glass blowers to make than flat or domed lids with finials.

The example pictured above was probably made by the Lockport Glass Works in Lockport, New York, during the mid-nineteenth century.

What is it worth?
This piece sold at auction in 2004 for $2,310.

item 6

"lily-pad" jug

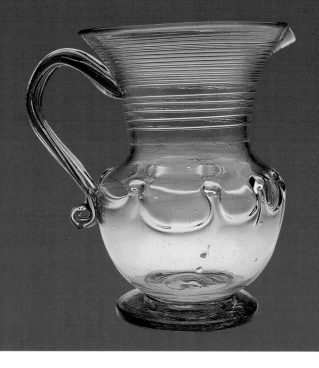

what is it? This pitcher or jug is in a classic American style that was first made in the glass houses located in southern New Jersey and is called a "lily-pad" jug. The glass made in this area is called "South Jersey" by collectors, but many of the glass makers from this area moved to New York State and took their techniques and decorative motifs with them.

It is said by many that the lily-pad design reached its zenith in New York State, and firms such as Redford, Redwood, Harrisburg, Lockport, Lancaster, Saratoga Mountain, and Ellenville made many of the finest examples of this type of ware. Lily-pad pieces are distinguished by the scallop or swag around the body of the pieces that was made by superimposing an additional gather of glass over the body that was applied and then hand tooled.

Valued at $11,000

7¾-inch-tall one-quart jug, with a squat globular body and an applied strap handle with a medial rib and a crimped terminal at the bottom. The mouth is circular with a slightly pulled-out pouring spout, and the base is circular with a rough pontil. The neck is threaded, and there is a raised swag or wave-like decoration around the globular body. The glass is aquamarine in color and is unsigned. There is a faint ½-inch-long annealing fracture behind the lower terminal of the handle that does not break through the surface.

The South Jersey influence on this piece is seen not only in the lily pad but also in the threading around the jug's neck. Besides jugs, the lily-pad design can be found on covered sugar bowls, large open bowls, compotes, and vases. The examples made in New York State are largely aquamarine in color, but examples in deep sea green, blue, and amber are known.

The jug pictured above was made by the Redford Glass Works, which was located near Plattsburg, New York, or the Redwood Glass Works, which was near Watertown, New York. This is a fine example of this form, which has so much appeal for collectors of early American blown glass.

what is it worth? In 2005, this jug sold at auction for $11,000.

item 7

money box

Valued at $13,500

Money box or bank in clear colorless glass. Approximately 11¼ inches tall, this piece was constructed in five sections and assembled using "wafers" of glass to hold the various parts together. The goblet-shaped base is surmounted by arches formed from rods of glass. This construction is surmounted by a rooster sitting on the topmost wafer, and this gives the impression of the bird sitting on some sort of nest. The sides of the vessel are decorated with rigoree, and the knop above the arched rods is hollow and holds an 1843 dime.

what is it? Deming Jarves founded the Sandwich Manufacturing Company in Sandwich, Massachusetts, in 1825. One year later, the firm was incorporated as the Boston and Sandwich Glass Company. Jarves, who was born (according to some sources) on November 21, 1790, was the son of a prosperous Boston cabinetmaker. There is some thought that he may have trained in his father's enterprise, but the first notice of his working life came in 1813, when it was noted that the 22-year-old Deming was a partner in the "dry goods" firm of Henshaw and Jarves.

In 1817, Jarves became involved in the American glass industry when he and a group of associates acquired the property and facilities of the old Boston Porcelain and Glass Company in East Cambridge. They incorporated in 1818 as the New England Glass Company, and Jarves was listed as its "agent," which meant he was the general manager and sales agent.

After his father's death in 1823, Jarves went to Pittsburgh to visit the famed firm of Bakewell and Pears, and there he is said to have completed his education in the art and science of glass making. It was not long after this that Jarves' relationship with the New England Glass Company came to an end and he went to Sandwich, Massachusetts, to establish another factory. Jarves is said to have chosen Sandwich because he was "going to the fuel," which meant he was establishing his enterprise near a plentiful supply of wood that would keep the glass furnaces going. He may also have chosen this site because it was located on a body of water that made for easy transportation of goods to urban markets—particularly Boston.

The early pieces made by the Boston and Sandwich Glass Company were hand blown, and it has been said that the rarest examples of this early production are the banks or money boxes with rooster finials. There is one pictured in Ruth Webb Lee's *Sandwich Glass* (1939, published by the author, page 147), and both the one pictured by Lee and the one pictured here have a coin enclosed in the hollow top knop.

The one featured in Lee's book has an 1831 coin in it (denomination unknown), and the one pictured here has an 1843 dime. Some may think the coin itself is valuable, but in this case, it is not. An uncirculated 1843 dime is worth approximately $310, but the condition of this coin is not that pristine, and examples of 1843 dimes in lesser states are worth less than $50 each.

It is not unheard of for collectors to find pieces of glass with coins embedded in them by their glass makers as a dating device, but this is not a feature that is commonly found. These pieces tend to have been made after the seventeenth century, and most examples are European in origin. The ones associated with the Boston and Sandwich Company are generally from the 1830s, and the 1843 dime is one of the latest coins known to have been included in a Boston and Sandwich piece.

It is tempting to say that this piece was made in 1843 because of the dime, and it may very well have been. But the most accurate thing that can be said is that this particular bank could not have been made before 1843, and for safety's sake should be considered to be circa 1850.

The rooster was an important decorative theme at Sandwich, and besides sugar bowls and a few rare money boxes, Sandwich made a number of bird-watering devices that are surmounted by roosters. All of these are hard to find today, but the poultry watering bottles are the most common, followed by the sugar bowls, with the money boxes being the rarest.

what is it worth? This piece is such a rarity that pricing it is very difficult. It is not something that can be found at the corner antiques shop (as a general rule), and it is one of only a few of its kind known to exist. This particular example sold at auction in 2004 for $13,500.

item 8

syrup pitcher, "Rubina"

Valued at $350

Syrup pitcher with pewter top. The glass
shades from red at the top to clear at the
bottom, and the body has a raised flower
and leaf design.

what is it? This type of glass has a variety of names among collectors. Most call it "Rubina," but others might call it "Rubina Crystal" or spell the name "Rubena." Although this glass, which shades from transparent red to transparent clear colorless, resembles the "Amberina" glass that will be discussed next, it is different in that "Amberina" is a heat-shaded glass, while "Rubina" is not. "Rubina" was initially made to compete with "Amberina" and be a less expensive substitute.

To make Rubina, the glass blower starts by blowing a clear colorless glass vessel that is then flashed on the inside with a thin layer of red glass from the top to partway down the body, which makes the finished product appear to shade from red to clear. Sometimes the demarcation between the two colors is very subtle, but on other occasions, it almost looks as if there is a straight line between the areas of red and the clear colorless glass.

Rubina was first made in 1885 by George A. Duncan and Sons of Pittsburgh, Pennsylvania, but it was also made by the C. Dorflinger Glass Works of White Mill, Pennsylvania. The piece pictured was most likely manufactured by Duncan.

A similar type of glass is called "Rubina Verde," which is glass that shades from transparent red to a transparent light green that ranges from an aqua green to a yellow green. Like regular Rubina, the color shading is accomplished by flashing, and it too was made to compete with Amberina and be a cheaper substitute. This glass was reportedly made by the Boston and Sandwich Company and Hobbs, Brockunier of Wheeling, West Virginia.

Rubina can be found in a variety of forms that range from biscuit jars to candlesticks, cruets, butter dishes, jam jars, and perfume bottles. Bride's baskets in silver-plated frames are particularly desirable. Some pieces may be found decorated with enameled designs, and these are more valuable than similar pieces without the enameling.

what is it worth? Nineteenth- and early twentieth-century glass syrup pitchers with their original pewter tops have become difficult to find. Value this one at $350.

item 9

vase, "Amberina"

Valued at $350

Cylinder-shaped glass "vase" with a
square ruffled top. The glass shades
from a deep fuchsia at the top to a rich
amber at the bottom. This piece is
approximately 6½ inches tall. It has been
blown into a pattern mold.

what is it?

For centuries, glass makers were plagued with a particular problem. When they were making green bottles, the desired green color would change to red when the pieces were reheated toward the end of the manufacturing process to finish the lip or, later on, to remove some of the mold lines. This generally happened near the bottom of the glass batch in formulas that contained copper and iron, and when it occurred, the bottle was discarded in the "cullet" or scrap glass heap.

Glass makers considered this color change to be a great nuisance until Joseph Locke at the New England Glass Company had a better idea. On July 24, 1883, he patented "Amberina," which added a very small amount of gold to a formula for high-quality transparent amber glass. When portions of this glass were reheated, the gold caused the reheated portion to turn bright red, creating a bicolored ware that normally shaded from red at the top to amber. Rarely, the bottom was made to change colors to red, and these wares are called "reverse Amberina."

There is a highly romantic myth that Amberina originated when a glass worker (sometimes it is Joseph Locke, and sometimes it is someone named Andrew Long) accidentally dropped his gold wedding ring onto a parison of amber glass at the end of his blow pipe (alternately, the ring is dropped into the whole batch of glass). This is absurd and did not happen—in fact, could not have happened.

To affect the color change, the gold has to be in a special state, namely a solution of aqua regia (a volatile mixture of hydrochloric and nitric acid that will dissolve gold and platinum), and then be colloidally suspended throughout the glass batch. This is the only way the glass can be sensitized, and a gold wedding ring would only melt in the hot glass and leave a "button" of metal in the bottom of the batch and not materially change the chemical composition of the glass.

Amberina was the first of the heat-shaded glasswares to be marketed by American glass makers, and it was a big commercial success. The New England Glass Company made Amberina items by blowing, pressing, and blowing into molds. Rarely, they used Amberina for cut glass, and even more rarely as an outer layer over opal glass for what is called "plated Amberina."

The vase illustrated was blown into a mold with a diamond pattern that is called "Diamond Quilted" or "Venetian Diamond." There is no question that it was blown because there is a very distinct polished pontil on the bottom, and it was made circa 1885. There are some who would call this a "celery vase" because it was intended to hold this vegetable on the sideboard or dinner table. At the end of the nineteenth century, celery was considered an exotic vegetable and something of a status symbol in upscale Victorian homes.

Many other companies were quick to produce Amberina, including the Mt. Washington Glass Company of New Bedford, Massachusetts, which called its product "Rose Amber." Other companies used such names as "Ruby Amber," and competition caused New England to sue to protect its patent but also to lower the prices on Amberina products. It should be noted that when New England closed in 1888, the formula for Amberina went with the Libbeys to their new factory in Toledo, Ohio, and the Libbey Glass Company produced a very fine and highly regarded line of Amberina around the year 1900.

New England's Amberina was sometimes marked with a paper label, but most of these have disappeared over the years, and the majority of New England Amberina is therefore unmarked. Libbey, however, generally marked its pieces with the name "Libbey" in script.

Collectors need to beware because reproduction pieces of Amberina outnumber original examples by a wide margin. Always look for honest wear on the bottoms of genuine pieces. This type of wear consists of tiny, short, crisscrossing scratches as opposed to long parallel scratches, which are artificially induced by rubbing the bottom over a rough surface. In addition, reproductions may have a frosted pontil, modern shapes, and/or poor color.

what is it worth? The richness of the color of the Amberina greatly affects the value, as does the form. This example has good, dark rich color, but it is a rather commonly found form and should be valued at $350.

item 10

pitcher, "plated Amberina"

Valued at $12,000

Pitcher made from two layers of glass. The inside is white with a slight bluish or chartreuse cast, and the exterior is a deep fuchsia shading to an amber yellow. The globular body of the 7-inch-tall pitcher is ribbed, and the handle is a transparent amber.

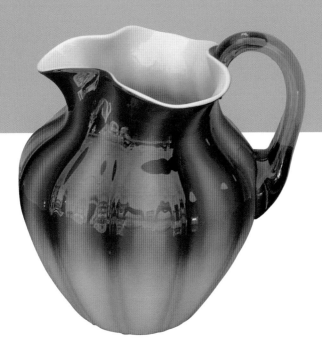

what is it? This is the rarest form of Amberina and is called "plated Amberina." It is rare not only because of limited production but also because it is extremely fragile and few of the pieces that were made have survived to the present day.

Plated Amberina was patented June 15, 1886, and it was made by plating a layer of opal glass with Amberina. This ware was always blown into a ribbed mold, and this is very important because reproductions—of which there are many—were not often made in this telltale ribbed mold.

Plated Amberina closely resembles Wheeling Peach Blow, but Wheeling Peach Blow was never made in a ribbed mold. In addition, the lining of genuine New England plated Amberina is never pure white. It has a sort of chartreuse (some sources say "bluish") cast that is unmistakable, while the modern copies usually have linings that are chalky or "dead" white.

Plated Amberina can be found in shapes that range from punch cups and tumblers to pitchers, spooners (spoon holders), toothpick holders, and syrup pitchers.

what is it worth? Finding a piece of New England Glass Company plated Amberina is a dream come true for collectors of Victorian colored art glass. This water pitcher is worth $12,000.

item 11

vase in stand,
Wheeling Peach Blow

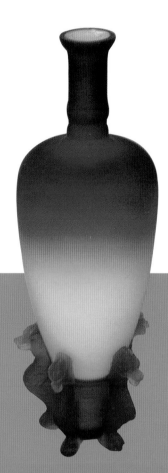

Valued at $2,000;
vase alone: $1,500

Vase in separate amber glass stand.
Both pieces together are 10 inches tall
(the vase is 8 inches while the holder
is 2 inches tall). The vase itself shades
from a rich mahogany red to yellow and
is shaped in the manner of a Chinese
ceramic vessel of the eighteenth century.

what is it? There is no doubt that this vase is a copy of sorts—but it is also a copy that is highly desirable to collectors, who refer to it with the somewhat strange sounding appellation of "Wheeling Peach Blow."

The Hobbs, Brockunier Company of Wheeling, West Virginia, was a large glass company that made an amazingly wide variety of glassware. The company manufactured everything from bottles and a range of pressed glass tableware to some fancy, high-quality blown glass pieces.

One of these lines was originally called "Coral," but the name was soon changed to "peach blow." There is some disagreement about the origins of this ware, with some people saying that Hobbs, Brockunier's "Coral" was based on a glass that was first exported to the United States by England's Thomas Webb Company in 1885 and was called "Peach Glass."

The Webb product was a heat-shaded glass that went from red on the top to yellow on the bottom. When the first shipment of this glass arrived in this country, a specimen was reportedly rushed to Wheeling, where Hobbs, Brockunier copied it and had it on the American market before the next boat from England could cross the Atlantic with more of the Thomas Webb heat-shaded glassware.

Other accounts of the creations of peach blow glass at Wheeling leave this part of the story out and start with the sale of personal property in the estate of Mrs. Mary Morgan, which happened March 8, 1886. At that sale, a Chinese "peach blow" porcelain vase with its stand sold for the then-astronomical sum of $18,000.

Art critics pooh-poohed this piece as being the "plug-ugly of ceramic art," and there was such a furor over the piece that the people who bought it stored it for fifty years before they would display it. Despite the disapproval of the art community, the American public was much taken with this peach blow vase, and it became an extremely popular symbol of opulence and wealth.

Companies came out with a peach blow this and a peach blow that, and one cosmetics company even marketed a line of "peach blow" cosmetics. The ever competitive Hobbs, Brockunier Company lost no time in producing a copy of the famous Morgan vase using its "Coral" color for the vase portion and amber glass for the griffin holder. It marketed this product as "Peach Blow."

Wheeling (or Hobbs, Brockunier's) "Peach Blow" or "Coral" is a very distinctive glass. It has an opal glass (white) interior lining that is cased with an amber-colored glass that contains colloidal gold salts. When the objects are reheated at the glory hole, which is an opening in the side of a glass furnace where the reheating of a glass object takes place, the part that is reheated turns a bright cherry red while the part that is not reheated remains a yellow to golden amber.

This is called "heat-shaded" glass, and in old examples there should be no clearly visible demarcation between the two color zones. In other words, there should be no visible line where one color stops and the other begins, and the colors should truly shade into one another. It is important to note that Wheeling Peach Blow is the only American made peach blow that is cased and consists of two layers of glass.

Like the other American-made peach blow glasses, Wheeling Peach Blow came in a satin and a glossy finish. The example of the Morgan vase pictured here is satin, which means its surface was given a kind of satiny, grainy finish by exposing the glass to hydrofluoric acid.

what is it worth? This circa-1886 vase and holder should be valued for insurance purposes at $2,000. Without the holder, the vase is valued at $1,500.

Related Item

Bicolored pitcher, 8 inches tall with square top, amber handle, and satin finish.

What is it?
Wheeling Peach Blow pitcher, circa 1890.

What is it worth?
$2,800

item 12

pitcher, New England Peach Blow

Valued at $850

Tankard style pitcher, 8½ inches tall, made from a single-layer glass that shades from a soft pink to white. The slightly off-color white handle is extruded into an attractive ribbed shape.

what is it?

On March 2, 1886, Edward Libbey of the New England Glass Company, which was located in Cambridge, Massachusetts, patented a glass that was heat shaded from a delicate pink to white. This effect was achieved by combining opal glass and gold-ruby glass in one pot, and, after a vessel was formed, reheating one part to make the glass turn a delicate pink while leaving the rest white.

This was a somewhat novel process because most heat-sensitive glasses were mixed in one pot, while this one was two separate glass mixtures that were commingled. The difference in manufacturing technique may sound a bit like splitting hairs, but it was enough to get Libbey and New England a patent for the glass that they called "Wild Rose" or "Peach Blow."

New England produced "Wild Rose" in several finishes, including satin and glossy (the piece pictured has a satin finish). It was also used as a base for "Agata" glass. "Agata" was a decorating technique patented by Joseph Locke on January 18, 1887, and in this process, "Wild Rose" was covered with a metallic stain or mineral color that was then exposed to a volatile liquid such as benzene or alcohol.

This left the surface mottled in soft colors against the background of rose shading to white. This surface decoration was then fixed in a muffle, which is a box made from fire-clay. The purpose of the box was to protect the glass item inside from being exposed to the flame and smoke when the box was placed in a muffle kiln to heat at 700 to 900 degrees centigrade in order to make the colors permanent.

"Agata" pieces were almost always left with a glossy surface, and satin-finished examples are considered to be rare. It should be noted that the "Agata" process could also be used on other types of glass, particularly an opaque green.

Both "Wild Rose" and "Agata" were made for only a short time because the factory closed in 1888 and moved to Ohio, where it became known as the Libbey Glass Company, which is still in business. "Wild Rose" can also be found with gilded and enameled decoration, which enhances the value.

what is it worth?

"Wild Rose" was made in some quantity and is perhaps the least expensive of the three major types of American "Peach Blow" glass. This particular satin finish pitcher should be valued at $850.

Tumbler, 3⅝ inches tall. The glass shades from pink to white and has a glossy, mottled effect over the entire surface. The base has a polished pontil, and the piece is unsigned.

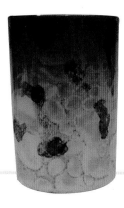

What is it?

The "Agata" decoration on New England Peach Blow is very rare and can be found on pitchers, tumblers, spooners, vases, punch cups, toothpick holders, mugs, condiment sets, and bowls. The color on the example pictured above is very strong and desirable.

What is it worth?

This tumbler sold at auction in 2003 for $1,050.

item 13

tumbler, "Green Opaque"

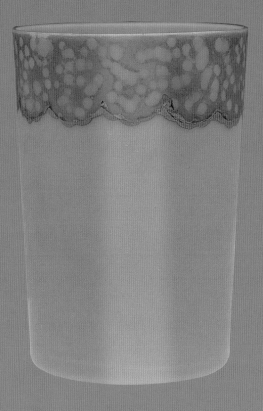

Valued at $600

Tumbler, 3¾ inches tall. The glass is an opaque green with a mottled blue decoration around the top that is separated from the rest of the glass with a wavy gold line. The piece is unsigned.

what is it? This tumbler is a fine example of the New England Glass Company's "Green Opaque," which was manufactured for less than one year. Introduced in 1887, it was made by adding a small amount of copper oxide to a batch of opal glass.

The resulting color is very distinctive, but Green Opaque is further distinguished by the blue mottled band that is found at the top of an object or around its midsection. As in "Agata," which is discussed above, this mottling is a metallic stain fixed with a firing in a muffle. Unlike "Agata," the decoration on "Green Opaque" is in the form of a band that is separated from the rest of the glass with a gold wavy line.

"Green Opaque" is almost always found in a satin finish, but glossy examples were made. Items made from "Green Opaque" include lamps, sugar bowls, pitchers, vases, cruets, punch cups, mugs, toothpick holders, condiment sets, and, of course, tumblers. These pieces are always unsigned, but occasionally, an example with a paper label will turn up.

what is it worth? This tumbler sold at auction in 2003 for $600.

item 14

pitcher, Mt. Washington Peach Blow

Valued at $35,000

Pitcher with a body that has a satin finish and a handle with a glossy finish. It is 7 inches tall, and the glass shades from a soft dusty blue to a soft dusty rose. On the body, in enamel colors, are painted depictions of daisies and a poem in ornate script by James Montgomery:

On waste and woodland, rock and plain
Its humble buds unheeded rise;
The rose has but a summer reign,
The daisy never dies!

what is it? The Mt. Washington Glass Company of New Bedford, Massachusetts, began making a heat-shaded glassware called "Burmese" in 1885. It contained uranium oxide and gold and shaded from a soft dusty rose to a pale yellow. In 1886, Mt. Washington's Frederick S. Shirley decided to modify the Burmese formula by adding cobalt oxide to the mixture, and the resulting product shaded from a pale dusty blue to a pale dusty rose.

On July 20, 1886, Shirley filed trade-name papers for the terms "Peach Blow" and "Peach Skin" and received the exclusive right to use these names. At the time, it was thought that anything marketed as "Peach Blow" would be a commercial success, but Mt. Washington's single-layer blue- to pink-shaded version did not sell well because the subtle coloration did not appeal to Victorian tastes, and comparatively little was made.

Mt. Washington Peach Blow can be found in both satin and glossy finishes, and it was produced in much the same shapes as the company's Burmese glass. Examples can be found decorated with enamel designs as well as gilding and glass house–applied ornaments, but these are all relatively uncommon. Examples with poems enameled on them, such as the pitcher pictured above, are extremely rare, and this piece is one of only a few known.

The poem found on this piece is the work of British/Scottish poet James Montgomery, who lived from 1771 to 1854, and was the son of a Moravian pastor. This particular verse has also been found on a piece of New England Wild Rose Peach Blow. Montgomery became the editor of the *Sheffield Iris* and served two terms in prison for writing political articles that did not find favor with the government. He is most famous for his approximately 400 hymns and is sometimes referred to as "The Christian Poet" or "The Conscientious Poet."

Many reproductions were made of Mt. Washington Peach Blow. Most of these have colors that are too strong to be part of the original production and have rough broken pontils that would have been ground down by Mt. Washington.

what is it worth? It is hard to determine the exact insurance replacement value of this piece because of the rarity, but it should be approximately $35,000.

item 15

biscuit jar,
"Royal Flemish"

Valued at $2,900

Covered jar in silver-plated frame. The
piece is 10½ inches tall at its tallest
point, and the glass has a satin finish.
The decoration is floral (pansies) and
hand painted with gilded highlights. The
top of the jar has a raised border that is
gilded. The metal frame is marked "James
W. Tufts Boston Quadruple Plate," and
there is a pair of tongs attached. The
glass itself is unmarked.

Paper label sometimes found on Mt. Washington's "Royal Flemish" wares.

Printed mark often found on Mt. Washington's "Royal Flemish" wares.

what is it? The glass portion of this piece was made by the Mt. Washington Glass Company of New Bedford, Massachusetts, and it is a type of glassware called "Royal Flemish." This product was patented February 27, 1894, by Alfred Steffin, who was head of the Mt. Washington decorating department. There is, however, evidence that this type of glassware was made by Mt. Washington as early as 1889.

"Royal Flemish" starts with a clear glass blank that is given an acid bath to create a frosted or satin finish. In many cases (but not all), the glass is then divided into irregular sections with heavy, raised gold lines, and the sections are filled in (again, usually but not always) with mineral stains that are commonly found in shades of brown, dark red (or maroon), dark green, and/or tan. This gave the surface a sort of stained glass window effect that was then decorated with raised designs that ran the gamut from representations of pseudoancient coins to heraldic devices and flowers.

Mt. Washington made a wide variety of pieces in its "Royal Flemish" line, and some of them were very atypical. This is one of those that departs from the usual "Royal Flemish" style decoration, but a very similar piece is attributed to the "Royal Flemish" line in Betty B. Sisk's authoritative book *Mt. Washington Art Glass Plus Webb Burmese* (page 192).

The frame was made by James W. Tufts of Boston, Massachusetts, who started his working career as an apprentice in a drugstore and ended up owning three apothecaries of his own. Tufts became interested in the soda fountain business and the equipment that was needed to run this sort of enterprise efficiently.

He started manufacturing items to be used in pharmacies and soda fountains, and in 1875, he began making other silver-plated items, such as the frame found supporting this "Royal Flemish" jar. This sort of frame with its pair of tongs was designed to hold a pickle castor.

The lid on this piece may be a replacement because the hook at the top was designed to hold the lid while the pickles were being extracted with the tongs. This particular lid, however, will not hang from this hook. It should be noted that Mt. Washington glass items are generally found with mountings from the Pairpoint Corporation or mountings manufactured by Mt. Washington itself. The Pairpoint Corporation was located next door to Mt. Washington and later purchased the glass company. Silver-plated items made by Mt. Washington itself are generally marked with an "M.W."

Tufts is noted for his very high-quality silver-plated wares. The phrase "quadruple plate" used in the mark refers to the amount of silver used during the plating process. "Quadruple plate" is the thickest plate commonly found on American silver, and the only one that is thicker is called "Federal specifications."

what is it worth? This piece sold at auction early in 2003 for $2,900.

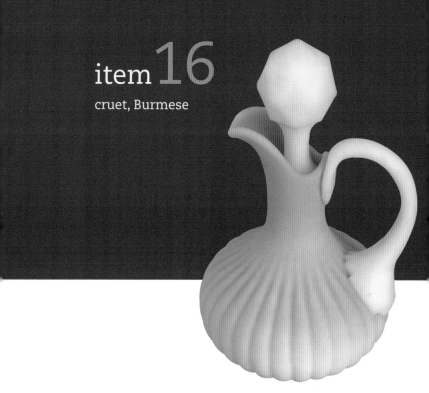

item 16
cruet, Burmese

what is it? The formula for this glass includes white sand, lead oxide, purified potash, niter, bicarbonate of soda, feldspar, fluorspar, uranium oxide, and just a pinch of gold (about one and a half pennyweights for every hundred pounds of white sand). When this is mixed together and heated, it produces a glass that is a lovely soft yellow. However, when this yellow glass is returned to the opening in the glass furnace called the "glory hole" and reheated, the portion of the yellow that is exposed to the heat turns a soft salmon pink.

This type of heat-shaded glass is called "Burmese," and the formula was patented by Frederick S. Shirley of the Mt. Washington Glass Company on December 15, 1885. According to legend, this glass got its name when a beautiful tea set decorated with enameled flowers and leaves made from solid gold beads was presented to Queen Victoria, who reportedly exclaimed that the yellow shading to rose ware looked exactly like a "Burmese sunrise."

Mt. Washington licensed the Burmese formula to Thomas Webb and Sons of Stourbridge, England, who made the product under the trade name "Queen's Burmese Ware." Much of Webb's Burmese was marked with this designation on a paper label or in-

Valued at $1,400

Stoppered cruet, approximately 6 inches tall with a ribbed body. The glass itself shades from a soft pink at the top to yellow at the bottom. It has a satin finish.

cised into the glass, but the Burmese made by Mt. Washington was never signed.

Burmese was made with both glossy and satin finishes, and many of the finer pieces are elaborately enameled and gilded. Some of the more desired patterns include flying ducks as well as pieces in the Egyptian, Etruscan, and Persian manner. Beware: In the mid- to late twentieth century, pieces of old Burmese that were originally undecorated had some of these elaborate enameled decorations added by fakers in order to greatly increase their monetary value. Unfortunately, in many cases, the fakers did an excellent job of simulating the old decorating style, and telling old from new requires careful examination and familiarity with genuine pieces.

Over the past forty years, Burmese has been widely reproduced, particularly in Italy during the 1960s and '70s. These reproductions are usually easy to spot because the colors are much too garish, with the pink portion resembling liquid bubble gum instead of the soft salmon pink of the originals. In addition, the pontils on reproductions are often not as they would have been on the original pieces, with frosting occurring inside the pontil area or with jagged scars that would not have been left by Mt. Washington or Thomas Webb.

what is it worth? This circa-1890 Mt. Washington Glass Company Burmese cruet is worth $1,400.

item 17

vase, "Napoli"

Valued at $2,090

Vase, $3\frac{1}{2}$ inches tall and $4\frac{1}{2}$ inches in diameter at the rim. The piece is hand painted with representations of spider mums and gold tracery. The body has molded ribs, and the base has a polished pontil. It is signed "Napoli 623."

what is it? In 1894, Mt. Washington's Albert Steffin patented a new way to decorate glassware, and this new product was called "Napoli." "Napoli" is a clear colorless glass that is decorated with hand-painted colored enamels on the interior, but then the design is outlined on the exterior surface.

This is a sort of reverse painting on glass, and this technique tended to give the design more depth. In addition, this method allowed the piece to be fired only once to affix the decoration. In other techniques when gold and silver are used with enamels, they have to be fired separately because the enamels will sometimes absorb the precious metal if they are fired together. In "Napoli," the gold and the silver could be neatly separated and only one firing was required.

"Napoli" is found on shapes that were also used to make "Royal Flemish," and the two very different types of glass are sometimes associated with one another. The relationship between the two can be seen in the gold tracery on this vase, which closely resembles that found on "Royal Flemish."

With its characteristic wide flaring rim, the vase is given a special name and is usually referred to as a "sweat pea" vase after the flower that it was designed to hold. In the past, "Napoli" has been somewhat undervalued, but prices are now rising.

what is it worth? This piece sold at auction in 2004 for $2,090.

item 18

bowl, "Crown Milano"

what is it? Glass manufacturers have been decorating white glass blanks with hand-painted designs for centuries, and in the late nineteenth century, many European glass houses were producing these white wares with a satin finish and elaborate painting. In the United States, the Mt. Washington Glass Company produced its own version of this ware that is considered to be among its most elegant and beautiful lines.

On July 6, 1886, Frederick Shirley and Albert Steffin were given a patent for a method of decorating white glassware that involved using a stencil and a bag of powered carbon or a brush. The process started with an opal glass blank that was free blown, blown in mold, or pressed.

Valued at $2,200

Tri-cornered bowl in a silver-plated stand. The piece is 12 inches tall overall, and the bowl is 10 by 12 inches. The base glass is opal that has been decorated with polychrome pansies. The stand has three feet and is ornamented with vintage (bunches of grapes) and floral motifs. The bowl has a polished pontil and is signed in red with "C M" under a crown and the number "63." The stand is marked with a "P" inside a diamond.

The blank was first given an acid bath to give the surface a satin finish and then a stencil with a prepunched design was placed over the surface and dusted with the carbon from the bag. This left an outline of the desired decoration on the surface that the decorators could follow when they were applying the colors and gold embellishments.

One of several marks found on Mt. Washington's "Crown Milano" wares.

Sometimes, these decorations could be quite elaborate, and the glass blanks often had prunts and/or elaborate handles and finials. This ware initially was called "Albertine," but the name was changed to "Crown Milano" because it sounded more impressive. It is thought by some that the name alone made this product a commercial success.

"Crown Milano" is normally found signed like the piece pictured, but some pieces were marked with a paper label, most of which have been lost over the years. As a result, most of these pieces will be unmarked.

The silver-plated stand that supports this piece was made by the Pairpoint Manufacturing Company, which was founded in 1880 and located next door to Mt. Washington in New Bedford, Massachusetts. Pairpoint purchased Mt. Washington in 1894 and established the Pairpoint Glass Works, which remained in business until 1938. The silver plating on this stand is very worn, but that does not greatly diminish the overall value of the piece.

This particular object is called a "bride's basket" or "bride's bowl" because pieces in this shape were favorite gifts to Victorian brides. Other "bride's baskets" have bail handles, and the one pictured was probably meant to serve as a table centerpiece or fruit compote.

what is it worth?
Bride's baskets are highly desired by collectors as are pieces of "Crown Milano." This example, however, has a decoration that is rather restrained for this genre, and this simplicity is not in its favor. The insurance replacement value of this piece is $2,200.

item 19
pitcher, "Overshot"

Valued at $400

Water pitcher with bulbous body and square top with an applied, extruded handle. The glass is blue shaded to clear colorless with an uneven almost "pebbly" surface that is rough to the touch.

what is it?

This type of glass is called "overshot," and in this particular case, it was made by blowing a clear glass parison and then fusing a blue glass rod to the area where the upper portion of the finished pitcher would be. This was then manipulated so that the upper area was colored by the blue rod while the bottom portion stayed clear. This is called the "die-away" or "die-castaway" method, and it is the simplest way to achieve bicolored ware that is not heat shaded.

Next, the piece was rolled over the marver (an iron, wood, or marble table) that had been covered with very small fragments or shards of glass. The hot surface of the glass picked up the tiny pieces as the parison was rolled over the marver and then the gather was slightly reheated and finished. Sometimes, this process was used in conjunction with the craquelle method, where a bubble is blown into a gather of molten glass and then the mass is plunged into ice water, causing the parison to "crackle" or fracture.

In the minds of some collectors, "overshot" glass is associated with the Boston and Sandwich Glass Company of Sandwich, Massachusetts, but many other companies made it, including the Reading Artistic Glass Company of Reading, Pennsylvania, and the Portland Glass Company of Portland, Maine, to name just a few. This type of glassware was also extensively made in European glass houses, and the example illustrated may be American, but it may also be European in origin. A positive attribution is impossible, but rightly or wrongly, many collectors would assume it to be American.

Although it was made somewhat earlier, "overshot" glass was first very popular during the last quarter of the nineteenth century, and this piece should be dated circa 1885.

what is it worth?

Victorian water pitchers made using the die-castaway method are fairly common, but the "overshot" surface of this piece helps raise the monetary value of this example to $400.

item 20

bowl, Mt. Washington cameo

Valued at $1,500

Bowl, 8 inches in diameter.

The base glass is white with a pink layer over the top in the form of a lady in silhouette surrounded by a wreath of flowers, ribbons, and butterflies. There is a polished pontil on the bottom, and the ribbon is scalloped and pointed. The condition of the piece is good except for a minor flake on the rim.

what is it? This bowl has been decorated to bring to mind a Victorian cameo—but the piece is not "cameo glass." Cameo glass is created by carving through one or more layers of glass to create a design (pictorial or geometric) that contrasts with the base layer. This piece was made by using an acid cut-back method, which is sometimes referred to as "acid etched cameo."

When the Mt. Washington Glass Company made this piece, it started with a gather of opal glass that was then dipped in pink or rose glass to give the opal glass a pink casing. After the piece was blown and shaped, it was covered with an acid resistant wax and the design was cut into this, exposing the pink glass below.

Next, the piece was given an acid bath, and the pink on the places where the wax had been cut away dissolved and disappeared, leaving the image that is seen in the picture on the previous page. This is not a decorative technique that is widely associated with nineteenth-century American glass houses, but Mt. Washington made it in shades of pink and white, pale blue and white, greenish blue and white, and light green and white. The pink is the most commonly seen.

what is it worth? The chip on the rim—even as minor as it is—adversely affects the value of this bowl. Its insurance replacement value in this condition is $1,200, but in perfect condition, the value would be at least $1,500.

item 21

pitcher, "Pomona"

Valued at $800

Tankard pitcher, 8½ inches tall with
frosted and mineral-stained surface.
The mineral stains are in shades of
yellow, gold, and blue. There are yellow
bands at the top and bottom and a
depiction of berries, leaves, and stems
around the body.

what is it? In mythology, "Pomona" is the name of the Roman goddess of fruit trees, but this is also the name given to a type of glassware made by the New England Glass Company of Cambridge, Massachusetts. It was first patented by Joseph Locke on April 28, 1885, and was originally made using a rather complicated labor-intensive process.

Pomona started with clear, colorless crystal glass that was blown into a vessel of the desired shape using the usual methods. After it was shaped, the surface of the piece was covered with wax or some other acid-resisting material. Next, young women cut large numbers of curved lines through the wax with etching needles, which created a frosted crosshatched effect when the vessel was immersed in acid.

The design also was cut into the surface at this time—most commonly it was a leaf and berry motif like the one seen in the piece pictured above, but other more elaborate designs such as grapes and leaves and even butterflies with sheaves of wheat or pansies were created as well. A clear, unfrosted band generally was left at the top of each piece and sometimes around the bottom.

After the piece had been immersed in acid, the engraved lines and decorations took on a frosted finish. Next, the decoration and the top rim (and sometimes the bottom) were colored with mineral pigments to make them stand out against the background. As might be expected, this was a very labor intensive process, and Locke was soon looking for a way to achieve much the same effect but at a lower production cost.

The method arrived at was patented June 15, 1886, and in this process, the areas that were to remain unfrosted were covered with an acid-resistant material while the rest of the body was covered with some sort of powered resin that protected the surface from the acid to a certain point. However, it allowed the body to become stippled or frosted, eliminating the need for the young women to engrave all those lines.

Collectors call the first method of making Pomona "First Ground" or "First Grind," and the second process is called "Second Ground" or "Second Grind"—and of course, "First Ground" is preferred to "Second Ground." The piece illustrated here is "Second Ground" and has a very typical decoration for this type of ware.

what is it worth? Pomona glass is not easy to find in
the current antiques market, but "Second Ground" pieces are
much more commonly encountered than "First Ground" examples. This particular "Second Ground" pitcher is a commonly seen
form and has some wear to the mineral colors. It should be valued
at $800. A similar "First Ground" example normally would be
$200 to $250 more.

Related item

Pomona tumble-up, two pieces with
an overall height of 8½ inches. Both
pieces have a pontil and a frosted
background with a subtle diamond
pattern throughout the bodies. Both
are decorated with a band of light
blue flowers and leaves, but the
tumbler has a scalloped gold rim
around its top.

What is it?
A tumble-up is simply a carafe with
a tumbler used as a cover for the
open mouth of the lower container.
These were used in bedrooms to
hold water so that if people wanted
a drink during the night, they had it at hand and did not have to go all the
way to the kitchen or—heaven forbid—the pump out back.

This "Second Ground" or "Second Grind" Pomona glass tumble-up has a
very typical cornflower decoration that is seen on many pieces of this
genre. What is not typical is the "Diamond Optic" pattern that was
achieved by blowing these pieces into a mold.

What is it worth?
The form of this piece and molded pattern make it valuable, and early in
2005, this item sold at auction for $4,510.

item 22

vase, "Mary Gregory"

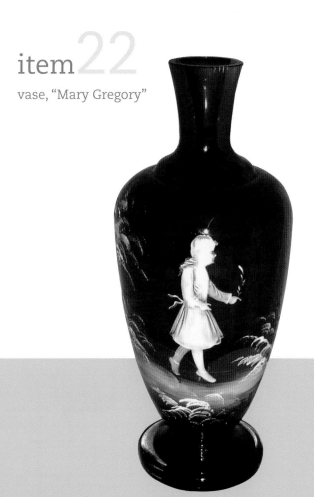

Valued at $275

Free blown footed vase with classical amphora shape tapering to a slender flaring neck. The glass is cranberry in color and is decorated with a white enameled depiction of a young girl holding a sprig of vegetation in her hand, done in silhouette style. The vase itself is 9½ inches tall.

what is it? It is a great mystery why this type of glass is called "Mary Gregory." It is just one of those myths that began, assumed a life of its own, and now refuses to fade away.

There is no doubt that there was a woman named Mary Gregory who worked for a brief time (some sources say as little as two years, others ascribe a longer tenure of up to ten years) at the Boston and Sandwich Glass Company in Sandwich, Massachusetts. Current research suggests that she specialized in painting scenes with animals and did not decorate any glass whatsoever with the images of children dressed in Victorian garb.

In any event, the glass that now bears her name originated in Europe, probably in the third quarter of the nineteenth century. The images generally depicted children—both boys and girls—engaging in childhood activities such as rolling a hoop, playing badminton, catching butterflies, playing musical instruments, or just carrying flowers. Pieces may also feature cherubs, and we have seen one example with decoration that can be described only as a depiction of a leprechaun. For the most part, collectors like pieces with a lot of activity, and there is demand for examples with children doing unusual things such as riding bicycles.

"Mary Gregory" glass came in a variety of colors. The least desirable of these are clear and amber followed up the scale by green, blue, amethyst, and cranberry. Of the final two colors, amethyst is probably the rarest hue, but cranberry is the most desired by current collectors and commands the highest prices (with all other factors such as the nature of the decoration being equal).

Although "Mary Gregory" glass originated in Europe, American glass houses also made this ware. It is said that "Mary Gregory" pieces made in Europe (primarily Italy, England, and Bohemia) can be distinguished by a small amount of tinting on the face or clothing or by the use of gilding. American pieces are said to be all white with no trace of tinting or gold embellishment, but this is open to some debate.

"Mary Gregory" glass was made right up to the turn of the twentieth century, and the piece illustrated above is possibly American circa 1885. Be aware of new reproductions that feature screen-printed designs—these can usually be detected with a magnifying glass—and that lack honest wear on the base of the glass.

what is it worth? "Mary Gregory" is relatively plentiful, and this vase is worth $275.

item 23

vase, "Mother-of-Pearl Satin Glass"

Valued at $400

7½-inch-tall vase with a bulbous body and a flaring funnel shaped neck and lip. The body is raspberry colored over a white lining and has diamond designs throughout. The rim is amber, and the piece has a satin-finished surface with a neatly polished pontil on the base.

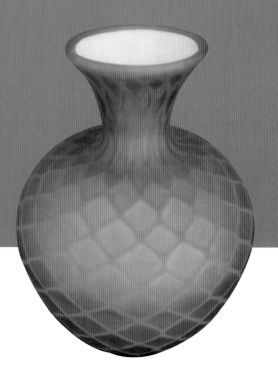

what is it? This type of glass has a number of names including "Pearl Satin Glass," "Pearl Ware," and the one most often used by American collectors, "Mother-of-Pearl Satin Glass." This type of glass was really the invention of Englishman Benjamin Richardson, who patented the process in 1857.

It involved blowing a gather of glass into a patterned mold in which the design was protruding. This left indentions in the glass body, and when the gather was dipped into another batch of glass, air was trapped between the two layers in these indentions. After this, the piece was immersed in hydrofluoric acid to roughen up the surface and give it a satin-like finish.

The finished product has a wonderful shimmering, almost underwater appearance that is very attractive and soon became popular with the consuming public. Great quantities of mother-of-pearl satin glass were made in Great Britain, Bohemia, and the United States. It was most popular during the last quarter of the nineteenth century.

The piece illustrated is circa 1885 and has a diamond quilted pattern. This means that the interior of the mold had raised diamonds arranged in neat rows, and when the white glass, which is now seen as a lining, was blown into this mold, the diamond forms were pressed into the surface of the white inner layer. The raspberry-colored outer layer was then plated on top of the white, trapping air between the raspberry layer and the white layer in the diamond shapes. Raspberry is a very desirable color to collectors, but the diamond design is commonly found.

The amber rod of glass around the rim suggests that this piece might have been made by Hobbs, Brockunier but that should not be considered to be a firm attribution. The polished pontil indicates an American or British origin, while a piece with a rough, unpolished pontil is often Bohemian.

what is it worth? The popularity of mother-of-pearl satin glass has been declining over the past two decades or so and, as a consequence, prices have declined as well. Years ago, this vase might have commanded as much as $600, but today the price is down to a bit more than half that at just $400.

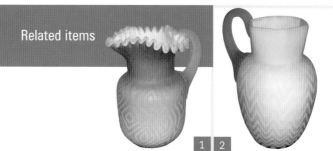

Related items

1 Mother-of-pearl satin glass pitcher with a white lining and apricot glass top layer that shades from dark to light. The piece is 8 inches tall and has a ruffled triangular top and extruded clear glass handle that has been frosted or given a satin finish. The air trap design is composed of squares within squares, and the piece has a polished pontil.

What is it?
The air-trap pattern on this piece of mother-of-pearl satin glass is called "moiré" after moiré or watered silk that the pattern is said to resemble. This piece has a polished pontil and is probably British.

What is it worth?
With the rarer moiré design, this pitcher should be valued at $500.

2 8-inches-tall mother-of-pearl satin glass pitcher with octagonal top and clear, extruded handle that has been given a satin finish. The inner layer is white with an air-trap design that is a series of inverted "V's" joined together, and the outer layer is yellow shaded to clear using the "die-away" method that was discussed earlier. The piece has a rough pontil.

What is it?
The air-trap pattern on this mother-of-pearl satin glass pitcher is called herringbone, and the origin of this piece is probably Bohemia circa 1890.

What is it worth?
The herringbone pattern is rather commonly seen in mother-of-pearl satin glass, and Bohemian-made examples of satin glass are not as highly regarded (for the most part) as those made in the United States or Great Britain. Because of these factors, the value is $400.

item24

ewer, "Rainbow Mother-of-Pearl"

Valued at $750

Decorative ewer or pitcher with a handle in the manner of ancient Etruscan vessels. The handle is frosted clear glass, and the bulbous body has dimples in the side. The white lower layer is striped with broad ribbons of pale blue and pink, and it has been pattern molded with circular air traps. The piece is 7 inches tall at its tallest part (top of the handle to the base), and the pontil is polished.

what is it?

This is a special type of mother-of-pearl satin glass that is called "rainbow mother-of-pearl." It is relatively rare and a variety of satin glass that is highly desired by collectors.

Rainbow mother-of-pearl was made much like other mother-of-pearl satin glass with a white inner layer that was pattern molded—in this case with a pattern that is sometimes called "raindrop" or "coin spot." After the piece has been molded, rods of colored glass are laid across the parison to give the striped effect and then the entire piece is cased in clear colorless glass.

The best rainbow mother-of-pearl pieces have more than two colors, with the most commonly found hues being pink, blue, and yellow. It is also a plus if the colors are bright and bold, but the hues found on the piece illustrated are rather subtle and can be hard to see. It should be pointed out, however, that the reproductions of this type of glass generally have colors that are too bold and brash, and this is a telltale sign that the piece is not an original.

The somewhat neoclassical form of this particular rainbow mother-of-pearl example is very attractive and is much in its favor. The polished pontil and the form suggest that this piece was probably made in England circa 1880.

what is it worth?

With three colors instead of two, this piece would have been worth well over $1,000, but with only two subtle shades the value is $750.

item 25

pitcher, Tiffany

Valued at $3,500

8½-inch-tall pitcher decorated with a
cut and engraved vintage pattern
consisting of grape clusters, leaves, and
vines. The pitcher is a waisted cylinder
with an applied handle and a polished
pontil. The glass itself is a deep blue with
an iridized finish, and it is signed on the
bottom "L C Tiffany Favrile."

what is it? Louis Comfort Tiffany was the son of Charles Lewis Tiffany, who, along with Charles Young, founded a store in New York City in 1837 to sell stationary and bric-a-brac including Chinese fans, desks, silverware, and umbrellas. The firm was originally known as Tiffany and Young, but the name was changed to Tiffany and Company in 1853.

Louis Comfort Tiffany was born in 1848, and his family hoped that he would follow his father into the family business, but the younger Tiffany had other ideas. He was primarily interested in painting; he studied painting in Paris under the American artist George Innes and painted in Europe and Morocco.

Upon returning to New York City, the younger Tiffany entered into the field of applied arts and became an interior designer to the "upper crust." In 1881, he was commissioned by President Chester A. Arthur to redecorate the state apartments in the White House, and he began having such items as wallpaper, fireplace tiles, and decorative accessories manufactured to suit his taste and design ideas.

L.C. Tiffany was involved with a series of companies that started with the Tiffany Glass Company, which was founded in 1885, and the Tiffany Glass and Decorating Company, which was incorporated in 1892. This latter firm was established to manufacture a variety of objects to be used in the decorating business in addition to selling furniture and church fittings (such as stained glass windows).

In 1893, Tiffany became president of the Stourbridge Glass Company of Corona, Long Island, New York, and in 1902, the name of this company was changed to "Tiffany Furnaces." This company had been started by Arthur J. Nash (and others), and it was Nash who perfected the lustered, iridized glass technique that is often associated with Tiffany Glass.

The color of this lustered ware depends on the color of the base glass on which it is used. When, for example, it is applied to a transparent yellow glass that is comparable in color to olive oil, the resulting surface has a golden appearance. When the base glass was cobalt blue, like the piece illustrated above, the result was a brilliant, metallic blue with an iridized surface.

This is particularly apparent on this piece because the top luster has been cut through with a vintage pattern to expose the cobalt blue base glass underneath that looks dark against the metallic blue surface. The term "Favrile," found as part of the mark on this piece, is Tiffany's trade name, and it was derived from the Latin for "handmade" or from the Old English for "belonging to a craftsman." It should also be noted that the term was originally spelled "Febrile," but "Favrile" soon became the spelling of choice.

This piece was probably made circa 1910, and at one time, it probably had a set of tumblers with it that have now disappeared. Buyers should be very wary of both blue and gold Tiffany lustered glass because fraudulent pieces now greatly outnumber genuine pieces. A number of late-twentieth-century companies made this type of glass, and all unscrupulous people had to do to turn one of these modern pieces into a "Tiffany" was to scratch a few initials and maybe the word "Favrile" on the bottom with a diamond-point stylus. This kind of fakery is just too easy, and large numbers of fraudulently signed pieces of this type of glass do exist. Anyone thinking of purchasing a piece signed "Tiffany" should get advice from a specialist before buying.

what is it worth? Gold and blue lustered Favrile are among the most common of all the Tiffany glass found. Gold, however, is far more common than blue, and this pitcher should be valued at $3,500.

Related item

Small gold iridescent vase with polished pontil. This piece has dimpled sides, a slightly flared rim, and is 1¾ inches tall. It is signed "L. C. T. R3798."

What is it?
Tiffany gold Favrile glass is the most commonly found type of Tiffany glass. It was made in relatively large quantities and is still readily available to collectors.

The original purpose of this diminutive piece of glass is open to some debate. It may have been a toothpick holder but might also have been designed to be a violet vase. In any event, it is a charming little piece and the kind that often starts a collection of Tiffany glass.

What is it worth?
$450

item 26

vase, Tiffany flower form

Valued at $8,500

13¼-inch-tall vase in the form of a flower with opalescent top and decorated with depictions of green leaves. The piece is signed "LCT R9785."

what is it? The early history of the Tiffany Glass Company has been discussed above, and the undecorated lustered wares were among the simplest and most prolific of Tiffany's creations. Tiffany and his glass workers created a wide range of glassware that was in some cases designed to imitate ancient glass that had been buried in the ground for millennia, but they also tried to imitate the decorations found on ancient glass items that were made in places such as Egypt and Cyprus.

The variety of Tiffany glass is stunning, and some of his most attractive pieces are called "flower form" vases because they were made to resemble—in a rather abstract way—flowers blooming on long stems with circular domed bases. Tiffany was a major proponent of the American Art Nouveau movement, which drew much of its inspiration from the sensuous curves and tendrils found in nature, and these Art Nouveau designs often feature overblown blossoms. Tiffany's flower forms were a veritable garden of tall and elegant but entirely fanciful blooms that existed only in the mind of the Tiffany designers and craftsmen, never in nature.

Flower form vases are usually found in sizes that range from 10 inches to a towering 18 inches tall. Generally, the tall stems have swellings along their lengths to suggest the joints or knees found in living vegetation, and many pieces are internally decorated

with depictions of feathery looking leaves. The example pictured here is rather typical, although the floral cup is a little deeper than most and the top is plain rather than ruffled or notched as it often is.

There are few reproductions of Tiffany flower form vases, but always be wary of pieces that have little wear on the bottom and no provenance.

what is it worth? Flower forms are very desirable to collectors, and this one is valued at $8,500.

Vase, 9 inches tall, gold lustered glass with green and gold decoration around the bulbous top of the vase that resembles philodendron leaves and vines. The piece has a domed circular foot with a polished pontil. It is signed "1117 9459M L. C. Tiffany - Inc. Favrile."

What is it?

This is a small Tiffany flower form that is very elegantly decorated with leaves that were created by putting a dot of colored glass on the surface and then pulling a tool down the center to create the leaf form. This is much the same technique used by a dessert chef to decorate a plate or confection using dots of a fruit sauce and then running a knife or tool through the center to make a heart or a leaf.

What is it worth?

$6,500

Valued at $850

Bowl, 5⅞-inch diameter. The glass is light green with a white opalescent feather pattern. The base has a polished pontil and is signed "L. C. T. Favrile."

what is it? This type of Tiffany glass started out with a body of sensitive opalescent clear colorless glass that was then partially plated or flashed with another color. It is reported that L. C. Tiffany did not like this type of glass because it was being too widely used, and he considered it to be "too commercial."

This glass was made rather late in the history of Tiffany Studios, and it can be found in a variety of colors and patterns. Among the colors are ruby or pink, blue, lavender, yellow, brown, and green. The most commonly found pattern is probably "Rib," but examples in "Diamond," "Laurel," and "Dot" can be found as well.

Tiffany called this "Flashed Glass," but today's collectors usually refer to it as "Tiffany Pastel." This type of glass is commonly found in table wares, and it is interesting to note that Tiffany did not normally sign plates around the pontil as he did with many other items. Instead, plates are normally signed around the rim—and sometimes this signature is missed because people are looking in the wrong place.

what is it worth? This small bowl is very attractive and has an insurance replacement value of $850.

vase, Steuben "Aurene"

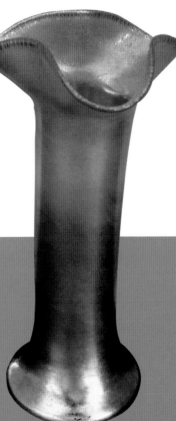

Valued at $950

Vase with a bulbous base and a cylindrical body that terminates in a flaring tricorn top. The body is amber in color and has a gold iridescence on the outer surface. It is 6 inches tall and is signed around the polished pontil "Aurene 141."

Mark found on this Steuben "Aurene" bowl surrounding the polished pontil.

what is it?

"Aurene" is the name that Frederick Carder of the Steuben Glass Works gave to his lustered glass that is very similar in appearance to Tiffany's "Favrile." In fact, Tiffany sued Steuben and Carder in 1913, saying Steuben had hired away one of Tiffany's old employees, who had given away the trade secret to making Favrile glass. The complaint went on to allege that it was difficult to distinguish between the Tiffany and the "imitation," or Steuben's "Aurene"—and indeed it can be. Tiffany dropped the suit in 1914.

Carder was an Englishman who worked for the prestigious Stevens and Williams Glass Company of Brierley Hill, England, but in 1903, he was sent on a fact-finding tour of the American glass houses by the South Staffordshire County Council. Initially, Carder was not enchanted with the United States and called it "Yankeeland." He vented his anger on the train trip to Corning, New York, by ranting to an elderly white-haired stranger who traded him acerbic quip for acerbic quip. That stranger turned out to be Mark Twain.

Carder's relationship with his employer, Stevens and Williams, had soured, and upon arriving in Corning, Carder signed an agreement with T.G. Hawkes, who had run an important glass decorating house in Corning since 1880, to start up a new factory that would be called the Steuben Glass Works (Steuben was the name of the county in which Corning was located). Carder planned to use an English staff to make his glass, but union trouble forced him to make other plans. When the factory opened in late 1903, many of the glass workers were Swedish.

Among Carder's first experiments was an attempt to learn how to make gold lustered glassware, and he registered his process on September 6, 1904, under the name "Aurene." The gold iridized finish was achieved by spraying the surface of an amber- or topaz-colored glass vessel with tin and iron chloride. Often, the spraying took place before the item was completely finished, and as the glass was further expanded, little fissures in the gold surface would develop.

Gold Aurene was very popular and was made until about 1933, but Steuben also developed Aurene glassware in different colors. Gold is by far the most commonly found Aurene color, followed by blue (which very closely resembles the Tiffany product of the same hue), then green, red, and brown. The last three are all quite rare and command very high prices.

It should be understood that Steuben marked its glass much more haphazardly than Tiffany. After a piece was made at Steuben, it went to the stockroom and stayed there until it was sold, at which time, the stockroom personnel would sign the piece either with a stamp dipped in acid or by incising "Aurene" with a diamond-tipped stylus. If it was a busy day, sometimes the clerks would just sign a few pieces here and there as time allowed and let the rest go unmarked.

Luckily for collectors, there is a company catalog that has line drawings of all Steuben products made between the factory's opening in 1903 and 1932. This catalog is very helpful in identifying unmarked Steuben, and it has been reprinted many times and is often part of any good book on Steuben glass.

The number 141 found on the bottom of the "Aurene" vase discussed above refers to its shape, and a quick check of the catalog shows that #141 is indeed this vase. This low number, along with the rather subtle gold coloring, suggests that this is a relatively early example of Steuben's "Aurene" and is circa 1910.

Again, there are many fraudulently signed pieces out there on the market, and buyers should take great care and check the catalog before making a significant investment.

what is it worth? Gold Aurene is the most common of the Steuben Aurene colors, and this vase is worth $950.

Related item

Steuben blue "Aurene" bowl with overall blue iridescence. It is 14½ inches in diameter and is supported on three feet. On the bottom, it is signed "Aurene 2586."

What is it?
A check of the Steuben catalog reveals that this is indeed the company's number 2586 bowl. It is blue Aurene, which is rarer and more valuable than the gold variety. This rather large circa 1920 bowl was used as a table centerpiece, and in many cases, it was used to float flowers such as gardenias. It was made after World War I.

What is it worth? $2,000

item 29

goblets, Steuben

what is it? It was difficult to have a financially successful glass company by manufacturing high-end art glass alone. Steuben relied on the sale of its lampshades, tableware, and lower-end decorative accessories to keep the firm in business.

This goblet is Steuben's number 6358 shape, and it was probably made circa 1930, just a few years before the company abandoned the making of colored glass in favor of crafting items only in clear colorless crystal. Over the years, Steuben made a number of blue transparent glasses including "Marine" blue, "Celeste" blue, and "Flemish" blue, but the blue of this goblet is called "French" blue.

The air bubbles seen on the bowl of this glass are not there by accident. When this goblet's bowl was made, the blue glass was blown into a mold that had little spikes that left the "controlled bubbles" decoration seen throughout the body. The random

Valued at $500

Pair of goblets in blue transparent glass with threading around the body of the glass and controlled bubbles throughout the body. The stems are supported on slightly domed feet, and each stem is wrapped with a rod of glass. One of the 7½-inch-tall goblets is signed with an acid etched stamp that includes the block signature that reads "Steuben." The other is not marked.

threading was done by taking a heated rod of "French" blue glass and pulling out a thin strand much as a candy maker might pull out tendrils of hot candy to make a spun sugar effect. This thread is wrapped around the most bulbous part of the bowl, and it is important to the value of these pieces that the threading be intact, as it is in this case.

Example of a mark often found etched into pieces of Steuben glass. Beware: This mark is easily faked.

what is it worth? These goblets were completely handmade and are very beautiful. It is very difficult today to find a pair of pre-1933 Steuben stems, and these two pieces should be valued at $500.

item 30

vase, Steuben acid cut back

what is it? As has already been said, many pieces of Steuben glass were not signed by the maker, and it is suggested that for identification purposes the Steuben catalog should be consulted. This is fine as far as it goes, but Steuben made hand-made glass, and variations of the shapes seen in the catalog do exist.

The first clue that this vase was made by Steuben is the translucent (almost opaque) green glass that Steuben called "green jade." Steuben made a number of jade colors including plum, yellow, blue (both light and dark), and rose, but the green jade seen here is by far the most plentiful.

Valued at $2,200

12-inch-tall green glass vase with cut decoration in a chrysanthemum and leaf pattern. The bottom has a polished pontil and a great deal of honest wear, but the piece is not signed.

The catalog reveals that the shape is Steuben (probably shape number 3278), but the double acid etched design (sometimes called "acid cut back" by collectors) on the piece is a combination of two Steuben patterns—"Chinese" and "Sculptured." The shield shaped border around the top is one that is generally found with the Chinese pattern, and the flower (chrysanthemum) and leaf pattern on the rest of the body is called "Sculptured."

This design was achieved by placing a pattern on the glass using a material that would resist the action of hydrofluoric acid, which would cut away the background, leaving a raised decoration that looks like it was sculpted into the glass. This type of decoration is very beautiful, but it is most desired when two layers of glass were used and the acid treatment left the design in one color juxtaposed against the other. This particular vase is circa 1925.

what is it worth? The fact that this piece is unsigned does not hurt its value, which is $2,200.

item31

vase, Steuben

Valued at $600

Three-pronged vase, 6¼ inches at tallest point. The glass is a rich transparent blue, and there is a polished pontil. This piece is unsigned.

what is it? This is a very strange-looking piece, and because it is unsigned, its origins are not readily apparent. However, a quick look at the Steuben catalog of line drawings will reveal that this is the 2744 "stump" vase. This form came in a variety of sizes and configurations.

The largest and most impressive is the number 2750, which has four prongs, with the tallest branch being 17 inches tall. There are two versions of the three-pronged variety pictured above, and these are the number 2743 and number 2744. The catalog identifies the number 2742 as having two "stumps" while the number 2741 has just one.

These unusual vases were made in a variety of colors including the iridescent gold "Aurene," but the one pictured above is in Steuben's "Celeste" blue. This piece was made circa 1920.

what is it worth? Collectors seem to be very fond of this form, and this one is worth $600.

item 32

vase, Durand

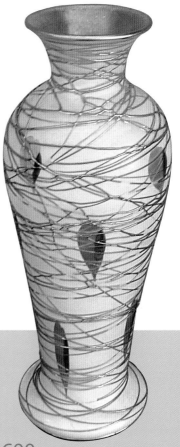

Valued at $1,600

9¾-inch-tall vase. The base glass is opal, and the piece has a flared lip with a throat that is lined with gold luster. The body itself is wound with gold threading. It is further decorated with bicolored gold and blue hearts. The bottom has a polished pontil, and the piece is unsigned.

what is it? At the tender age of 12, Victor Durand went to work at the famous factory Cristalleries de Baccarat in Baccarat, France. He was the fourth generation in his family to work for this important company, but shortly after Victor started at Baccarat, his father (who was also named Victor) decided to move to Millville, New Jersey, where he went to work in the glass factories that were located there.

The kind of mark sometimes found on pieces of Durand. The "6" indicates the height of the piece and the other number indicates the shape.

Young Victor and his family followed in 1884, and at the still-tender age of 14, he went to work at the Whitall-Tatum factory. After working in several other glass factories, Victor and his father leased the old Vineland Glass Manufacturing Company in Vineland, New Jersey. The previous owners of this facility had made bottles and jars, and the Durands initially made such things as glass rods and glass tubes to be used in thermometers.

Eventually, the elder Durand retired and Victor Jr. became the sole owner of the Vineland Flint Glass Works as well as the majority stockholder of three companies located in Vineland. The operation was huge, and it is said that the company produced as many as 40,000 thermos bottles a day—but Victor Durand Jr. had bigger and more artistic ideas.

In 1924, Martin Bach Jr. of the Quezal Art Glass and Decorating Company came to Vineland to teach the glass workers how to make artistic glassware. In December 1924, a shop was set up for this purpose. Initially, glass was made that looked very much like the products that were formerly made at Quezal, but as time passed, new colors and designs were added and Durand Art Glass took on a look all its own.

In 1926, Durand Art Glass was awarded the gold metal at the Philadelphia Sesquicentennial International Exposition. Unfortunately, Victor Durand Jr. died in an automobile accident in 1931 and the company was merged with the Kimble Glass Company. Art glass production at Vineland ceased shortly thereafter.

Durand made the standard lustered wares that were made at Tiffany, Steuben, and Quezal, but he also made elaborate crackle glass in Moorish and Egyptian patterns, as well as cut glass, among other things. The piece illustrated above is opal glass with a heart design in blue and gold. This was made by placing a small blob of glass on the surface and then pulling it with a hooked tool to form the heart (pastry chefs use a similar technique with dessert sauces).

The piece was then embellished with fine gold threads that are called "spider webbing," "spider," or "broken thread." Like the majority of all Durand glass, this piece is unsigned. Those that do have a signature have the name "Durand' in script or the name "Durand" written over a large "V." Interestingly, genuine Durand pieces that were unsigned in the factory often have had fake signatures added.

what is it worth? There is no question that this piece was made by Durand because of its form, style of decoration, and color. Major loss to the spider webbing could cause a significant reduction in price of up to 80 percent, but this piece is in near perfect condition. The value is $1,600.

Related item

Durand vase, 5½ inches tall, with dark blue lustered glass decorated with opal heart shapes and vines. Polish pontil signed "Durand" over a large "V" with "1722-6" below.

What is it?
Even if this vase were not signed, it would obviously be the product of Victor Durand's Vineland Flint Glass Works. The color is right, the shape is right, and the "heart and vine" (also called "heart and clinging vine") pattern is right.

This is a very standard pattern for Durand, and many, many examples can be found with this decoration. Durand glass such as this piece was retailed in jewelry stores and in upper-end department stores and was never inexpensive.

What is it worth?
This vase sold at auction early in 2005 for $1,265.

item 33

pitcher, Fenton

Valued at $350

9¾-inch-tall pitcher with ruffled top
and bulbous body. The glass is
transparent green with white accents at
the top and white circular areas
scattered throughout the body.
There is no pontil.

what is it?

The Fenton Art Glass Company was organized in 1905 by Frank Fenton and his brother, John. Frank Fenton was born in Indiana, Pennsylvania, in 1880, and upon graduating from high school apprenticed at the Indiana Glass Company. By 1898, he was a foreman, but before establishing his own company, he worked for several other glass houses, including the Jefferson Glass Company and the famous Northwood Glass Company of Wheeling, West Virginia.

According to Fenton family legend (the company is still very much in business in Williamstown, West Virginia), Frank and John started the business with just $284.86 (Frank had the $284, and John added the 86 cents). They first opened a decorating shop in Martins Ferry, Ohio, which bought blanks from other glass makers and added the embellishment.

In 1906, the decision was made to move the company to Williamstown, West Virginia, and to begin manufacturing glass. The first piece of glass was produced at the new Williamstown factory on January 2, 1907. John Fenton left the company in 1909 and established his own glass making firm in Millersburg, Ohio, and compared to the Fenton Art Glass Company, which is still in existence, this venture was very short lived.

Today, Fenton is best known for its carnival glass, which it first made shortly after the company moved to Williamstown. It made a wide variety of other glass including art glass, custard glass, slag glass, and mold blown opalescent pieces, of which the pitcher pictured above is a good example.

Opalescent glass was made by blowing a parison of colored glass and then coating it with a clear layer of glass that contained bone ash and arsenic. After this was done, the glass was blown into a mold that left raised areas on the glass body. When the piece was removed and reheated, the raised areas turned white against the colored background. The flat bottom on this piece, which has no pontil or polished area where a pontil might have been, attests to it having been mold blown.

In this case, the opalescent pattern is called "Coinspot" and has its origins in late Victorian glassware. This particular pitcher is shown in a circa 1910 Fenton catalog, and this piece can confuse collectors because it resembles items that were crafted at an earlier time (opalescent glass was first made in England in 1870).

what is it worth?

Fenton glass is very popular with collectors, and this piece is worth $350.

1 Opalescent syrup pitcher, 5¾ inches tall with original pewter top. The body is spherical with a short neck. The glass is transparent blue with white decoration of leaves and flowers.

What is it?
This type of Victorian opalescent syrup pitcher is in a pattern that collectors call "Daisy and Fern." Pieces with this pattern were made by a number of companies, including the Buckeye Glass Company in Martins Ferry, Ohio; the Jefferson Glass Company in Steubenville, Ohio; and the Northwood factory.

It is likely that one of the companies other than Northwood made this particular example because Northwood used a ribbed swirl mold on its "Daisy and Fern" items. The earliest date for this opalescent blown-in-mold pattern is 1888, and it was certainly made well into the first quarter of the twentieth century.

Syrup pitchers are highly desirable and can command premium prices. Many reproductions of this pattern were made, and buyers should look for honest wear and glass that is not slick or "greasy" to the touch.

What is it worth?
$375

2 Opalescent tankard pitcher, in blue transparent glass with white decoration of curved stripes at the top and stars at the bottom. The piece is 8¼ inches tall, and has a polished pontil.

What is it?
Opalescent glass came in an amazing variety of colors and patterns. This particular pattern is patriotic and called "Stars and Stripes" by collectors. When this pattern was originally made by the Hobbs, Brockunier Company of Wheeling, West Virginia, it was more prosaically called pattern "293."

Hobbs made this pattern from 1886 to 1894. It was then made by the Beaumont Glass Company of Martins Ferry, Ohio, after it acquired the molds from the defunct Hobbs. Original colors were cranberry, blue, and clear colorless. The "Stars and Stripes" pattern can be found on water pitchers, tumblers, barber bottles, and lamp globes.

Twentieth-century reproductions were made by Fenton and L.G. Wright, but this is an instance in which the reproductions have interest for collectors to a certain degree. New items were made in the form of a creamer, a cruet, a tumbler, and a barber bottle.

What is it worth?
This piece sold at auction in 2003 for $4,510 (a similar pitcher in cranberry sold for slightly more at $4,700).

item 34

pitcher, "Middle Period" cut glass

Valued at $715

8-inch-tall jug or pitcher in clear
colorless glass with a ribbed, solid
handle that terminates in a crimp. The
body is decorated with simple panels,
and the top edge is notched. The piece
has a polished pontil and is unsigned.

what is it?

This one-quart jug is a type of cut glass that is generally termed "Middle Period," and is said to have been in fashion from about 1830 to the time of the beginning of the American Brilliant Period, circa 1880. It is often distinguished by simple flute or panel cuts, and many novices do not recognize it as being actual cut glass. American Middle Period cut glass is sometimes distinguished by very fine engravings, but it is the flute cuts like those seen on the jug pictured above that are the most commonly found decoration.

This jug is thought to have been made at the Wheeling Flint Glass Works of J & C Ritchie. This firm had its beginnings in 1829 when John Ritchie and Jesse Wheat founded the Wheeling Flint Glass Works in Wheeling, West Virginia. They had high expectations for their new enterprise and advertised that their workmen were "of the first skill and taste." Ritchie and Wheat fell out in 1831, and Ritchie bought Wheat's interest (as well as those of an investor named Thompson).

After a year or so of struggle, Ritchie sold half the business to his brother, Craig Ritchie, and the business became J & C Ritchie. Their main competition in the area was the firm of Wheat, Price & Company, which had been established by Jesse Wheat (and others including John H. Price), after he left Ritchie and Wheat. In 1834, J & C Ritchie expanded by buying out Wheat, Price & Company.

In 1836, George W. Wilson became a partner and the name was changed to Ritchies & Wilson. The jug above was made between 1835 and 1837 and is very similar to a creamer that descended in the Ritchie family and currently resides in the Ogleby Institute Glass Museum in Wheeling, West Virginia.

what is it worth?

This piece sold at auction in April 2005 for $715.

American Glassware   85

item 35

water pitcher, red cut to clear

Valued at $1,200

8-inch-tall water pitcher with bulbous body. The glass is high-quality clear colorless lead crystal with an overlay of red glass. The body of the pitcher has been elaborately cut, allowing the clear glass to show through the contrasting colored layer.

what is it? Until the time of the American Centennial Exposition, which was held in Philadelphia in 1876, cut glass tended to consist of rather simple motifs such as panel cuts, flute cuts, concave diamond cuts, or maybe the strawberry-diamond and fan pattern. Copper wheel engraving was widely used as well, and the glass tended to be elegant, but it did not have the sparkle and jewel-like qualities of cut glass that was made from the late 1870s to about 1910.

This prismatic type of glass is called American Brilliant Period cut glass, and it gained popularity after the American public saw it exhibited at the Centennial Exposition. This glass was made with deep miter cuts, which at first were straight, but later could be curved. These deep "V" shaped incisions were arranged in elaborate patterns that were designed to catch and reflect the light just like the surface of a cut and polished diamond.

It is said that during the thirty-year American Brilliant Period, there were more than a thousand cutting shops making this type of highly faceted cut glass. Most used thick, high-quality lead crystal blanks and turned out elaborate pieces that were very expensive, but other cutting shops reportedly used ordinary pressed glass blanks and made cut glass of a somewhat lesser quality.

In its day, American Brilliant Period cut glass was one of the standard gifts that brides received. It was also an extremely popular gift for men to give to their wives and mothers on birthdays, anniversaries, and Christmas. This kind of cut glass was so pricey that few could afford to assemble a table service all at once, so a few pieces were bought at a time. An attempt was made by homeowners to build up extensive sets of stemware in a particular pattern as well as matching specialized tableware pieces such as punch bowls and ice cream services (an ice cream service consisted of a long, rectangular or oval platter and a set of smaller, shallow bowls).

The vast majority of all American Brilliant Period cut glass is made from clear colorless glass, but, rarely, examples can be found with a colored overlay that has been cut through to the clear. The most commonly seen colors are red or green (blue pieces do exist), and these "color-cut-to-clear" pieces are highly sought after by collectors. Monetarily, they are much more valuable than pieces with similar designs and quality of cutting that are just clear glass.

The pitcher pictured above is not signed but it has been attributed to C. (Christian) Dorflinger and Sons of White Mills, Pennsylvania, which was in business from 1881 to 1921. Dorflinger came to this country from France in 1846 and established a factory making lamp chimneys and lampshades in Brooklyn, New York, in 1852. In 1860, he founded the Greenpoint Glass Works (also in Brooklyn), which specialized in making cut glass, and this company was so highly regarded that it made a service for President Lincoln to use in the White House.

Dorflinger became ill and, in 1863, sold out his interests in the Brooklyn glass houses and moved to White Mills, Pennsylvania. By 1865, Dorflinger had recovered from his malady and founded the Wayne Country Glass Works to make fine flint glass. In 1881, Dorflinger entered into a partnership with his three sons (William, Louis, and Charles) to make cut glass. The company was named C. Dorflinger and Sons and made cut glass throughout the entire American Brilliant Period.

Dorflinger was known for its color-cut-to-clear pieces, and this example has a shape and design that is consistent with that attribution. American Brilliant Period color-cut-to-clear glass was tricky because in some cases, the design to be cut through the colored layer was so intricate that it would largely obliterate the colored overlay and leave nothing but the clear colorless base glass showing with just a little color peaking through here and there. In other words, to be effective, the design chosen to be used on an American Brilliant Period piece of color-cut-to-clear had to be such that it left behind enough color in the uncut places to form a pleasing contrast with the colorless base glass.

The particular pattern on this pitcher is very effective because the variety of motifs left behind form a very pleasing juxtaposition of the two colors. The large hobstars, for example, have been modified to have a bold section of "chair bottom" in the center (think of the design used to make the caning on a chair's seat), and this motif has hobnails that retain the red on their top, while the hobstar itself has the red in the points that surround the "chair bottom" design.

Novice collectors need to be very careful of reproductions because the vast majority of the pieces being offered for sale on today's market are reproductions. To distinguish new from old, remember that the cutting on new pieces is often somewhat sharper than that found on old examples, and the walls of the vessels are often thinner.

In addition, every surface on old American Brilliant Period cut glass was polished carefully so that no gray areas that were created by the cutting process were allowed to remain. On newer pieces, this polishing process is not as meticulous and gray areas are almost always left behind.

what is it worth? The prices of cut glass seem to have fallen over the past decade or so. We feel it is mainly because of the incredible number of reproductions that have appeared in the marketplace and because young collectors often find this type of ware to be a little fussy for their tastes. Still, cut glass is near and dear to the hearts of many, and this circa 1890 example is certainly a rarity that should be valued at $1,200.

item 36

bowl, American Brilliant Period cut glass

Valued at $450

Bowl, 8⅛ inches in diameter
and 3½ inches tall. High-quality, clear
colorless glass that has been cut.
There is some expected roughness
at the rim.

what is it? This master berry bowl (there were once a number of smaller, individual berry bowls that accompanied it) is in a pattern that was patented by the Hunt Glass Company of Corning, New York. This is its "Royal" pattern (patented by Harry S. Hunt on July 11, 1911, patent No. 41,555), a variant of the Famous "Russian" pattern, which was patented by the T.G. Hawkes Glass Company on June 20, 1882. Hunt's "Royal" pattern has a "Russian" design on the bottom and the "Arcadia" design on the sides ("Arcadia" was a pattern originated by the Sterling Glass Company of Cincinnati, Ohio).

The "Russian" pattern is a refinement of the old "Star and Hobnail" pattern, which was made as early as the 1860s, but the Hawkes' version was an arrangement of pyramidal stars and hobnails that some liken to the "Daisy and Button" pattern. Shortly after this pattern was patented, Hawkes was approached to make a glassware banquet service for the Russian embassy in Washing-

ton, D.C. This pattern was chosen and the name "Russian" was attached to it.

It should also be mentioned that another set of "Russian" glassware was made for the American embassy in St. Petersburg, Russia, and still another with the addition of an engraved eagle for the White House in our nation's capital. This was an extremely popular pattern, and, eventually, it was made by a large number of glass companies in a number of variations.

These include "Ambassador," "Canterbury," "Cleveland," "Persian," "Polar Star," and, of course, "Royal."

what is it worth? $450

item 37

carafe, American Brilliant Period cut glass

Valued at $600

7½-inch-tall carafe, clear colorless glass, cut in the American Brilliant Period style. It is not signed.

what is it? This water carafe is in the "Venetian" pattern, which was patented by T.G. Hawkes in 1890. It is a fairly hard-to-find pattern and was the first to use the Greek cross in cut glass design.

For Thomas Gibson Hawkes, cut glass was a family tradition that went back for five generations. He was born in Ireland in 1846, and his family had been glass cutters in England as well as in Waterford, Ireland.

Hawkes was trained as a civil engineer, and when he came to the United States in 1863, he went to work as a draftsman for John Hoare, who owned a glass-cutting shop in Brooklyn, New York. Hawkes moved to Corning, New York, in 1870 and continued to work for Hoare and Dailey in their other cutting operation, which was located in the Corning Glass Works.

Hawkes opened his own cutting operation in 1880, which he called "T.G. Hawkes Rich Cut-Glass Works" until about ten years later, when the name was changed to the more straightforward "T.G. Hawkes & Company." Hawkes' pieces were often signed with a trefoil with a fleur-de-lis in the center flanked by two hawks. On an earlier version, the name "Hawkes" appears above the fleur-de-lis.

These, like many of the signatures found on the cut glass made by many other companies, were applied using a stamp that was dipped in acid and applied to the surface. This left a faint gray mark that can be very hard to see. Collectors know to search diligently on the bottoms of pieces and under the handle to detect these hard-to-see marks, and they carefully view the piece from different angles under light trying to catch the telltale "wink" of the gray signature.

These signatures can also sometimes be detected by huffing breath over the surfaces where a signature might be lurking. Sometimes, the brief fog that is generated will reveal the almost invisible signature. Unfortunately, the piece pictured above was never signed.

what is it worth? $600

item 38

oval tray, Sinclaire cut glass

Valued at $600

Oval tray, 9¾ inches long by 6¼ inches wide. The glass is high-quality clear colorless, and the decoration is cut. The bottom has been polished, and there is no evidence of a pontil. It is unsigned.

what is it? In the 1880s, Henry Purdon Sinclaire Jr. went to work for Thomas G. Hawkes in his Corning, New York, glass house as a bookkeeper. Sinclaire was a bright young man, and he soon learned all about the glass making business. By 1888, Hawkes was so confident in Sinclaire's abilities that he left the twenty-five-year-old man in charge of the company whenever Hawkes traveled overseas.

Sinclaire was a physical fitness devotee, and after his hikes through the surrounding countryside, he would sketch some of the things he saw to be used in the decoration of glass. Hawkes is said to have encouraged Sinclaire but did not think that his designs for engraving glass were commercially feasible.

Sinclaire married in 1892, had a child, decided to open a china decorating shop, and used the trade name "Ravenwood" on his pieces. He continued to disagree with Hawkes about what kind of cut glass would sell, and he developed an antipathy toward Brilliant Period design and the art glass that Hawkes protégé Frederick Carder was making at Steuben.

He opened up his own engraving business in Corning in 1905 and began selling his pieces to fine retailers such as Tiffany in New York City and John Wanamaker in Philadelphia. He signed many of his wares with an "S" in a wreath or the name "Sinclaire" in capital letters. Collectors should beware, however, because this signature has been faked.

Sinclaire did make some Brilliant Period patterns, but he liked to combine these motifs with engraved decorations, as can be seen on the oval platter pictured above, which is in his "Silver Thread and Floral" pattern. The hobstars seen on the rim and in the center of this piece are heavily identified with American Brilliant Period pieces, but the engraved "silver thread" around the rim and the leaf and floral design in the center are a good example of Sinclaire's design.

Sinclaire died in 1927, and his company closed in 1929.

what is it worth? $600

item 39

pitcher with silver top, green cut to clear, intaglio

Valued at $7,425

11-inch-tall pitcher or jug with silver top and handle. The glass is transparent green that is dark green in the thicker areas and a lighter yellow green where the glass is thinner. The decoration is swirled panels with cut in flowers, leaves, and vines alternating with plain panels and between the two are notched ridges. The lid and handle are decorated with "C" scrolls. The glass is unsigned, but the lid is marked "Gorham Mfg. Co. Sterling 5."

what is it? Color cut to clear cut glass is rare, but just as rare, and in some cases rarer, is cut glass in a solid color other than "crystal" or clear colorless. Even harder to find is solid color cut glass that is intaglio cut and not cut in the prismatic designs that are normally associated with the American Brilliant Period.

The term "Intaglio" cut refers to deep copper wheel engraving done on the surface of glass that leaves an image below the top surface that is generally pictorial in nature. Sometimes, during the late nineteenth and early twentieth centuries, intaglio cutting was combined with prismatic motifs, and in the case of the jug pictured above, the notched prism cuts that separate the panels are of this latter type.

A claret jug was designed to hold a dry red table wine usually associated with the Bordeaux region of France. Sometimes it is fortified with brandy and served after dinner as a digestive or before dinner as an aperitif to stimulate the appetite. These vessels are very commonly English, but this one is a rare American example.

The glass on this piece is not signed, but the sterling silver one-piece top and handle were made by the Gorham Manufacturing Company of Providence, Rhode Island, which was founded in 1831 as Gorham and Webster. It did not become the Gorham Manufacturing Company until 1865 and kept that name until 1961, when it became the Gorham Corporation. Gorham is one of the most highly regarded of all the nineteenth- and twentieth-century makers of American silver, and it often made fittings for items made from glass or ceramic.

what is it worth? In 2004, this turn-of-the-twentieth-century claret jug sold for $7,425 at auction.

Intaglio cut glass vase, 5¾-inch-tall vase with flaring, scalloped rim. It is clear colorless glass with a decoration of leaves, vines, and grape clusters. It has a polished pontil and is unsigned.

What is it?

This "sweet pea" vase has an intaglio-cut decoration on it that is associated with the Tuthill Cut Glass Company of Middletown, New York, which was founded in 1900 as C.G. Tuthill and Company. The name change occurred in 1902.

Tuthill did not make its own glass blanks but reportedly bought them from the Corning Glass Works as well as Dorflinger and Pairpoint. Tuthill was a very small decorating company and employed fewer than twenty cutters and engravers. Most of the patterns were designed by Charles Tuthill, who had learned his craft at the prestigious T.G. Hawkes Glass Company of Corning, New York.

Tuthill was known for the quality of its work, and it is said that not only did it specify a specific formula for its glass but also that Susan Tuthill measured every piece with calipers before it went out to make sure the cutting was to the correct depth. Today, the company is principally known for its intaglio patterns with fruit and flower motifs, but examples can be found with designs such as butterflies, birds, and dragons.

Collectors prefer that Tuthill glass be signed, but the quality of the glass and the configuration of the design suggest that the piece pictured above can be attributed to this company. This particular piece was made circa 1910, and Tuthill went out of business in 1923.

What is it worth?

$450

item40
paperweight, Boston and Sandwich

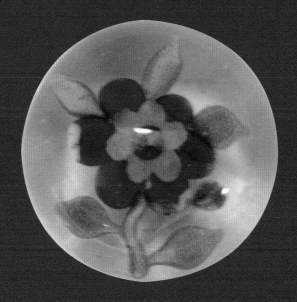

Valued at $1,200

Paperweight that is approximately
2¾ inches in diameter. The clear glass
dome surrounds a flower in shades of
opaque green, red, and yellow.

what is it?

The classical period for making paperweights in Europe was in the 1840s and 1850s, but in the United States, this art form developed a little later. Paperweights were made in this country in a number of glass houses, including Mt. Washington and the New England Glass Company, plus several firms in Pittsburgh, Pennsylvania, and New Jersey.

The weight pictured on the preceding page, however, was the work of Nicholas Lutz of the Boston and Sandwich Glass Company. Lutz was born in St. Louis, Lorraine, France, and learned the glass-making trade at the famous Cristalleries St. Louis, which was established in 1767 and was one of the foremost makers of French paperweights.

Lutz started working at Sandwich in 1869, and he remained there until the factory closed in 1888. Lutz specialized in making fancy and decorative items and is famous for the striped and threaded pieces that he did in the rather elaborate Venetian style. A number of glass companies in the United States and Europe made this sort of glass, and because none of these items was ever signed, a piece that meets this description is often called "Lutz-type."

A bit less familiar to many Sandwich collectors are the paperweights Lutz reportedly made after hours. They were never part of the Sandwich regular line of glassware, but they do turn up in the marketplace with some frequency (reports of people buying them for less than $50 are rather common because they are not recognized by many as being American, nineteenth century, and made at the famous Boston and Sandwich factory).

Lutz paperweights are distinguished by their lamp work inclusions of flowers, fruit, and vegetables. Lutz had special tools for producing the small pieces of glass that he used to make leaves and flower petals. He also made fruit such as apples, cherries, and pears as well as carrots. In addition, Lutz made paperweights with embedded crosses that were set among leaves.

The best of the Lutz paperweights have a latticino background, which consists of threads of glass composed into a sort of lacy base that has the fruit, flower, or cross placed above. Most of the Sandwich paperweights do not have this background and are only a single flower with leaves or a simple composition of fruits or vegetables and leaves.

Although the Chinese have produced pieces that might confuse someone who has never seen the real thing, reproductions are not a big problem with Boston and Sandwich paperweights. The modern Chinese weights are of very poor quality and have colors that would never have been used in the originals.

what is it worth? This very simple example of a Nicholas Lutz Boston and Sandwich paperweight is worth $1,200.

PRESSED
GLASS

item 41

salt, "Basket of Flowers"

what is it? This rectangular salt dip is in a "lacy" pattern made by the Boston and Sandwich Glass Company that is appropriately called "Basket of Flowers." The term "lacy" glass refers to a large group of Sandwich items that are distinguished by small raised dots in the background called "stippling."

Along with this raised-dot ground, there are depictions of flowers, foliage, rosettes, fleur-de-lis, and other similar motifs. The overall effect is said to be "lacy," and though this kind of glass was made at Sandwich, it was also made in Europe—particularly France—and in various American Midwestern glass houses.

Identifying the makers of these pieces is determined by their patterns, and researchers have spent years and years digging at Sandwich recovering broken pieces so that they can determine with some accuracy what was made there and what was not. Both

Valued at $10,450

Small rectangular dish, 3 inches long by 2⅛ inches tall. The glass is emerald green shading to a yellow green with a bit of red slag on the four feet. The decoration features a basket of flowers in the center with leaf scroll at the corners and above the feet. The ground of the piece is decorated with tiny raised dots. The piece is unsigned, and it is in good condition with the kind of relatively minor losses and flaking that are expected on glass of this type and age.

the New England Glass Company and the Jersey Glass Company made salts decorated with baskets of flowers, but there is no doubt that the salt pictured above was made at the Boston and Sandwich Glass Company.

These salts are most desirable (as a general rule) when they come in colored glass, and Sandwich used a relatively large number of colors to make its "lacy" salts. This is the only recorded example of this salt in this color, and that makes it a great rarity.

what is it worth? In 2004, this salt sold at auction for $10,450. Again, it should be pointed out that other "lacy" salts—especially those in clear colorless glass—may sell for less than 5 percent of this figure.

item 42

salt, "Lafayet"

Valued at $7,524

Small dish shaped like a side wheel
steam boat. The piece is 1½ inches tall
and 3½ inches long and has the word
"Lafayet" on the paddlewheel. There are
two four-pane windows on the stern and
a fleur-de-lis and scroll on the bottom.
The glass is fiery opalescent to opaque
mottled blue in light to medium shades.

what is it? On July 4, 1825, the first glass was blown at Sandwich, and this was also during the time that the French American Revolutionary War hero, the Marquis de Lafayette (1755–1834), was making a triumphal tour of the United States. At the time, there was an outpouring of souvenirs to commemorate the event, but interestingly, this small dish was not one of those objects.

The process of mechanically pressing glass into a mold was not an American invention, but Deming Jarves patented a type of machine with a plunger that revolutionized the process and made it much more practical for mass producing glass items. According to some sources, the actual inventor was a carpenter whose name has been lost to time. He wanted a certain piece of glass made (no one seems to know exactly what), and he went to Jarves to see if his company could do the job.

Jarves told him that it could not be done, but the carpenter persisted and asked if it was not possible to make a machine that could press glass into any desired shape. Jarvis agreed to see if it could be done and, together, he and the carpenter made a machine with a plunger that would help shape the glass in the mold.

The first machine was designed to make tumblers, and no one thought it would work. Fortunately for the Boston and Sandwich Glass Company, the first experiment was a success. The year was 1827, and research reveals that pressed glass may have been made at the New England Glass Company as early as 1826. In any event, Jarves patented his "improvement" in the method of pressing glass on December 1, 1828, but he and his company were actually pressing glass somewhat before that time.

The first mention of a "Lafayet" salt was that seven were made on March 9, 1827, and were sold for $1.16—or sixteen and one half cents each. Whether this reference is to the boat-shaped salt pictured above or to an oblong salt with the portraits of Washington and Lafayette (know as the "Washington-Lafayette salt") is open to some conjecture.

Small dishes such as this one are called "salts" or "individual salts" because they were used to serve this savory seasoning long before the salt shaker was invented. One of these was placed at each diner's place with a small spoon so that the person could take the amount desired and sprinkle it over his or her food. In addition, there were much larger vessels called "master salts" that were used to fill the smaller "individual salts."

Why the name "Lafayette" is misspelled "Lafayet" is a mystery that is unsolved and will probably remain so. In any event, this boat-shaped salt was made in clear glass, sapphire blue, opal, opaque blue, canary yellow, and probably other colors. The fiery opalescent to opaque mottled blue of this example is rare and unusual.

The Boston and Sandwich "Lafayet" salt came in a variety of designs. One has the word "Sandwich" on the inside of the base, and the same word on the underside of the base. Other varieties of this have "B. and S. Glass Company" on the end, but others do not. There are actually nine main categories of these "Lafayet" salts with seven subcategories, and all of these groupings indicate various variations in the "Lafayet" boat salt design. The example pictured above with the two four-pane windows on the stern is one of the rarest forms of the "Lafayet" boat salt, and very few are known to exist.

what is it worth? This salt sold at auction in September 2004 for $7,524. Other Boston and Sandwich "Lafayet" boat salts with more common designs and colors of glass sell for much less (some for less than $1,000).

item43

cup plate, "Chancellor Livingston"

Valued at $5,775

Small plate, 3⁷⁄₁₆ inches in diameter.
The rim is scalloped, and the border has
extensive stippling with a raised design
of shields, stars, hearts, and scrolls. The
interior design is of a side paddlewheel
boat with smokestacks and masts. The
glass is a deep, rich blue with an all-over
opal bloom. Two of the tips on the
scallops have been damaged; otherwise,
the piece is in excellent condition.

what is it? Collectors call this small plate a "cup plate," and there is some disagreement about its original usage on the table. One story holds that in the early to mid-nineteenth century, cups had deep saucers and our ancestors performed a ritual called "saucering."

When hot tea was served in the cup, it was poured into the deep saucer to allow it to cool, and this operation may have been performed more than once (i.e., pouring, the tea back and forth between cup and saucer). Finally, when the tea was cool enough, the wet cup was placed on one of these small plates so that it would not mar the surface of the table or stain the cloth and the beverage was drunk from the saucer.

Many specialists today doubt that this procedure was widespread in polite company, and though it may have been practiced in some areas, it was by no means ubiquitous. It is felt by many that these small plates were far more likely to have been used as butter plates. Whichever is true, it makes for interesting speculation.

Although glass "cup plates" were predated by earthenware examples, these small plates were made in some quantity at Boston and Sandwich and other American glass houses from about 1827 to 1850—or even a bit later. In fact, reproductions are still being made today.

"Cup plates" are usually divided into two categories: "historical" and "conventional." The "conventional" ones have motifs that are geometric or have depictions of flowers, stars, hearts, leaves, vines, and other such images. "Historical" examples are pictorial and depict the portrait of a person, the image of a place, or some historical event.

The historical "cup plate" pictured above is known as "Lee/Rose No. 631" and is attributed to the Boston and Sandwich Glass Company. The ship is the "Chancellor Livingston," which was named after Robert R. Livingston (1746–1813), who was a member of the Continental Congress and one of the five members of the committee appointed to draw up the Declaration of Independence.

Livingston negotiated the Louisiana Purchase and was chancellor of New York State from 1777 to 1801. He financed Robert Fulton in his steamboat ventures and for a while held a monopoly on Hudson River navigation.

This cup plate was made sometime between 1840 and 1845 and is in an unrecorded blue. It is thought to be unique.

what is it worth?
It is a bit hard to believe that such a small piece of glass could have a significant value, but this rare "lacy" cup plate sold at auction in 2004 for $5,775.

Related item

Small plate, 3⅜ inches in diameter. The plate has a scalloped edge with seventy-two scallops and an interior decoration of flowers and leaves. The color is a transparent emerald green. Two of the scallops on the rim have been broken off, and two other scallops have partially lost their tips. It is unsigned.

What is it?
This "cup plate" is known as "Lee/Rose No. 227." It is thought to have been made by the Union Glass Works of Philadelphia, Pennsylvania, and is very rare indeed, with fewer than a dozen known examples in various colors and edge variations.

What is it worth?
It sold at auction in 2003 for $6,500.

item 44

compote, "Princess Feather Medallion
and Basket of Flowers"

Valued at $19,800

Compote, 6 inches high with an oblong
bowl that is 9 by 10¾ inches. The edge of
the bowl is scalloped, and the interior
decoration is "lacy" with feather-like
scrolling and several baskets of flowers
among the various motifs. The stem is
eight lobed and has a leaf design. Bowl
and stem are attached with a wafer. The
glass is transparent canary yellow, and
chips have caused the loss or partial loss
of several scallops on the edge.

what is it? The pattern seen on this piece is called "Princess Feather Medallion and Basket of Flowers," and the bowl of this compote can be found used as a base for a covered vegetable dish. Interestingly, the vegetable dish has a cover, but the compote is never found covered. It is speculated that the reason for this is that when the dish was attached to the stem, it became so warped that the lid that was used on it when it was a vegetable bowl would not fit properly.

This compote is most commonly found in clear colorless glass, and in this type of glass, the pedestal bases that Sandwich used tended to vary in design from piece to piece. However, when this compote was made in a color other than clear colorless, the eight-lobed base pictured below is the one that was typically used.

The colors normally encountered for this particular form are canary yellow, light blue, sapphire blue, amethyst, and "Peacock" or blue/green. Any of these colored examples are considered to be great rarities.

what is it worth? In 2004, this compote sold at auction for $19,800.

item45

windowpane, lacy

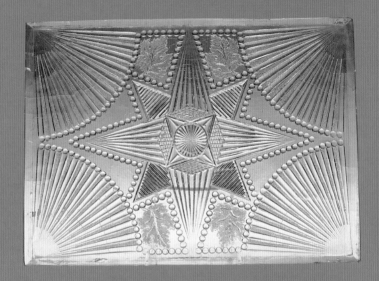

Valued at $12,650

Rectangular flat sheet of glass that is
13¾ by 9¾ inches. It is made from clear
colorless glass that is decorated with
fans, stars, and maple leaves, and there
is stippling in the alternating ribs of the
fans and all over the leaves.

It is in excellent condition with only a
few edge and corner flakes.

what is it? Eighteenth- and nineteenth-century American glass factories often stayed in business by making bottles and window glass, but although the bottles are highly collectible, the windowpanes have generally disappeared with the years. One of the exceptions to this is the "lacy" glass panes that were made by the Boston and Sandwich Glass Company and a number of other concerns in the Northeast and the Midwest—particularly firms in the Pittsburgh area such as Curling, Robertson & Company.

The exact origin of the pane pictured at left is open to some conjecture, but the current thinking is that it was indeed made by Boston and Sandwich. It has been exhibited at the museum in Sandwich, and it is thought to have been pressed sometime between 1835 and 1850.

The legendary glass specialist Ruth Webb Lee, in her book *Sandwich Glass*, speculated that windows such as this one were used on steamboats, but she also stated that they were used as doorway surrounds. This arrangement would have admitted a delightful play of light into the entryway while preserving the privacy of those inside.

This example is the largest of these panes that is currently known to exist. All of the early "lacy" panes are in clear colorless glass, but later panes of a different type can be found in color.

what is it worth? In 2004, this single windowpane sold for $12,650.

item46

vase, "Tulip"

Valued at $10,450

Vase, 10⅞ inches tall, 5¼-inch diameter at the rim, with two-piece construction. The upper vessel is attached to the hexagonal base with a disk of glass. The piece is a deep, transparent brilliant teal or blue-green with paneled sides and a deeply scalloped top. There are three chips that do not affect the aesthetic quality of the vase.

what is it?
Starting in the late 1830s, the Boston and Sandwich Glass Company began making vases in various colors. The piece pictured above is known to collectors as the "Tulip" vase, and examples can be found in canary yellow, several shades of blue, emerald green, amethyst, amber (very rarely), and a blue-green, known to some as "Peacock." Occasionally, the "Tulip" vase can be found in clear colorless, but many enthusiasts tend to prefer the colored examples.

Tulip vases are pressed glass, and they have a simple yet very elegant look. They are similar in shape and design to a pottery vase made in Bennington, Vermont, at a firm established by Judge Lyman Norton in 1831. This ware had a yellow or cream-colored body and was covered with a spattered brown glaze that collectors call "Rockingham" or "tortoise shell."

Sandwich made similar tall vases with scalloped or plain rims and deep bodies, but these related items had raised designs such as loops, large "thumbprints" (or "punties"), hearts, and swirled ribs. Bases on these pieces may be round, square, or hexagonal, and sometimes they are found mounted on marble bases.

Sandwich tended to mix and match tops and bases, and almost any type of top can be found fitted to almost any type of base. The "Tulip" vases are products of the 1840s, and the example pictured above is circa 1845 in the very desirable "Peacock" color.

what is it worth?
These vases can be very valuable, and even the slight damage does not impact the value by a great deal. This one sold at auction in May 2002 for $10,450.

item47

compote, open work

Valued at $17,600

Compote or open work fruit bowl, 8¼ inches tall by 8¼ inches in diameter. The rim has thirty-two points, and there are sixteen vertical staves in the body of the openwork bowl. The base of the bowl is a sloping thirty-four-point star that terminates in hexagonal knop and foot. Bowl and base are attached with a wafer, and the glass is a transparent amethyst. The condition is excellent with only one flake on the stem below the knop, which is thought to have occurred during the manufacturing process.

what is it? This rather unassuming compote or open work fruit basket is actually a great rarity. This nonlacy piece was made by the Boston and Sandwich Glass Company between 1840 and 1855, and few are known that are not severely damaged.

These pieces are not found in clear colorless glass. Most of the known examples are in this shade of amethyst, but peacock bluish/green is also known. The piece pictured above is typical of this genre except, at 8¼ inches, the diameter of the upper bowl is a little less than the typical 8¾ inches.

what is it worth? This open work fruit bowl sold at auction in 2004 for $17,600.

item 48

lamp base,
cut overlay

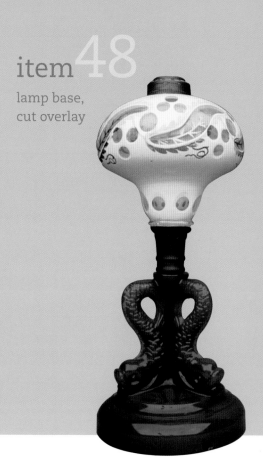

what is it? Starting in the 1860s, when kerosene oil began to supplant other types of fuel used for lighting, the Boston and Sandwich Glass Company began making fancy lamps that were decorated with "cut overlay." The base on this item is pressed, but the font was made by overlaying a blown, clear colorless glass parison with white glass and then cutting through the white to reveal the clear colorless layer underneath—thus, the name "cut overlay."

When there is only one layer of colored glass over the clear colorless under layer, it is said the piece is "plated," but when there are two layers over the clear colorless glass, the piece is said to be "double plated." "Plated" overlay pieces are far more common than "double plated" examples, and usually the double plate is a color such as red or blue over a layer of white. When the piece is cut, the white shows through only as an outline around the design and might be missed if the item is not carefully inspected.

Valued at $4,700

Lamp base composed of three dolphins on a two-step circular base. This base is connected to the font with a brass collar, and the font is clear colorless glass with a layer of white glass overlay. The white layer has been cut through to form circles, leaves, and berries. The base is semi-translucent "starch" blue, and the font is gilded. The piece is 11½ inches tall, has a chip on the side of the base, and there is an annealing crack in the tail of one of the dolphins.

The three-dolphin base on this piece is very unusual and desirable because few of the bases on these lamps are this graphically interesting. Most of the bases on these lamps were cut overlay like the font or made from brass or some simple form of pressed glass. A dolphin base such as this one is highly desired by collectors, and this particular base is only one example of the dolphin motif that was used by Sandwich on its glass items.

The leaf motif seen on the font is also rather unusual because most of the Sandwich cut overlay designs involved circles (or "punties"), quatrefoils, stars, ovals, and long panels. Sandwich also used cut overlay to make vases and cologne bottles.

what is it worth? This lamp base sold at auction in 2000 for $4,700.

item49

cream pitcher, "Ashburton"

Valued at $7,000

5¾-inch-tall cream pitcher in a
transparent canary yellow glass.
The solid handle has been applied and
has a crimped flourish at the end.
The base is flat and circular and there
is a polished pontil. The pattern consists
of a flute around the base with a
"thumbprint" above.

what is it? This piece is a little confusing because it is listed here in the pressed glass section yet the base clearly has a polished pontil. This is because this piece was molded but a pontil rod was attached to the bottom in order for the workman to apply the handle and to hand finish the top. When these operations were finished, the pontil rod was removed, leaving a scar that was subsequently polished smooth.

This pattern is called "Ashburton" or, far less commonly, "Ovington's Double Flute." It is also known as "Large Thumbprint" and a variety of other names that described variations in the pattern such as "Flaring Top Ashburton," "Barrel Ashburton," and "Near Slim Ashburton."

"Ashburton" is an early pressed glass pattern and is considered to be one of the classics. It was first made in the 1840s by the New England Glass Company of Cambridge, Massachusetts, but later it was also made by the Boston and Sandwich Company and McKee and Brothers of Pittsburgh.

"Ashburton" was largely made in clear colorless flint glass, but some later examples were made using a lesser quality glass, and these pieces are not nearly as desirable as the earlier flint glass production. Colored examples are all extremely rare, and only a handful of canary, emerald green, and fiery opalescent pieces are known.

"Ashburton" was extensively reproduced by the Libbey Glass Company of Toledo, Ohio (successors to the New England Glass Company), and the Westmoreland Glass Company of Grapeville, Pennsylvania. Museums such as the Metropolitan Museum in New York, the Smithsonian in Washington, D.C., the Henry Ford Museum in Dearborn, Michigan, and the Sandwich Glass Museum in Sandwich, Massachusetts, had reproductions made that were sold in their gift shops. Many of these reproductions were marked, but many of those that were not have been sold over the years as being originals. Buyers should use extreme caution.

what is it worth? This canary creamer may be unique. Certainly at the time it was sold at auction in 2002, it was the only recorded example of this creamer in this color and is the mate to the sugar bowl owned by the Glass Sandwich Museum. It sold at auction for $7,000. The insurance value of a similar creamer in clear colorless would be less than 5 percent of this price.

item 50

compote, "Ribbed Palm"

Valued at $600

$10\frac{1}{4}$-inch-tall open compote with scalloped rim. The background has a heavy, coarse ribbing with interspaced leaf forms. The hexagonal stem is hollow, and the base has a triple step with a simple circular foot. The base and bowl are joined together using a wafer, and the glass is clear colorless.

The piece is unsigned, and there are two flakes on the knop.

what is it? This open compote is in a pattern that is now universally called "Ribbed Palm," but when this design was first created, it was known as "Sprig." Over the years, it has also been called "Acanthus," "Leaf," and "Oak Leaf."

This pattern was patented April 21, 1863, by Frederick McKee of McKee and Brothers of Pittsburgh, Pennsylvania. Interestingly, a large number of "Ribbed Palm" shards have been excavated at the Boston and Sandwich factory, leading to the inescapable conclusion that this pattern was manufactured there as well.

Compared to "Bellflower," the ribbing found on "Ribbed Palm" is very wide and bold. The embossed palm leaves are very bold as well and provide a good handhold on the goblets. On "Ribbed

Palm" pieces that have handles, those handles are applied rather than molded on, and on those pieces with lids, the finials are in the shape of acorns.

The "Ribbed Palm" goblet has been widely reproduced, first in an assortment of colors by the L.G. Wright Glass Company of New Martinsville, West Virginia, and later by the Imperial Glass Company of Bellaire, Ohio, for Old Sturbridge Village in Sturbridge, Massachusetts. These latter pieces are marked "OSV." All of these goblets are lighter than the originals and are made from lesser-quality glass.

what is it worth? $600

item51

compote, "Horn of Plenty"

Valued at $3,500

Compote, oval bowl, 11¼ inches wide by 8¼ inches wide. The piece is 6¼ inches tall and made from clear colorless glass with a pattern that looks something like a cornucopia.
The edge of the bowl is scalloped, and the stem has six lobes. This compote was assembled using wafers.

what is it? This is another highly sought after pressed glass pattern. It has several names, including "Horn of Plenty," "Comet," and "Peacock Tail." It is most commonly found in clear colorless, but colors such as amethyst, canary, amber, blue, and clambroth, which is a grayish translucent glass said to resemble the color of the broth made from clams, turn up from time to time.

"Horn of Plenty" was made by several companies, including the Boston and Sandwich Glass Company of Sandwich, Massachusetts, and McKee and Brothers of Pittsburgh, Pennsylvania, (which used the name "Comet"). There is some disagreement as to when this pattern originated, with some sources saying the 1860s and others saying anytime between the 1830s and the 1850s.

"Horn of Plenty" is distinguished by a row of circular forms that trail long comma-shaped tails from their lower sections. The circles are of two types, and they alternate with one being a clear circle with a bull's-eye in the center placed alongside another circle that has raised diamond points in the center. The tails associated with the clear circles have raised diamond point decoration, and the circles with raised diamond points have bull's-eyes in the trailing tail.

This particular piece of "Horn or Plenty" was made by the Boston and Sandwich Glass Company sometime between 1850 and 1870 and is the largest of the open compotes in this pattern. It is a rare and hard-to-find form.

Reproductions of "Horn of Plenty" first appeared in the 1930s, and collectors need to be particularly careful with tumblers, goblets, and oil lamps.

what is it worth? This very rare open compote sold at auction in 2002 for $3,500. The most common "Horn of Plenty" forms in clear colorless glass can be worth less than $200 each.

Two-piece covered butter dish, 5 inches tall and 6 inches in diameter. "Horn of Plenty" pattern. The glass is transparent clear colorless, and the finial is in the image of a gentleman in a wig.

What is it?
This butter dish is called "Horn of Plenty with Washington Head." This is a fairly uncommon form that features the supposed image of the father of our country.

What is it worth?
This piece sold at auction in 2002 for $2,600. (Note: We have seen this piece quoted in recent price guides for as little as $500, which is far too low for this highly desirable piece.)

item52

compote, "Three Face"

Valued at $660

Open compote on tall standard, the stem of which is decorated with the image of three faces that resemble those of Victorian women. The standard is frosted, and the bowl it supports is clear with an etched design of flowers and leaves. The bowl has a scalloped rim and paneled sides. The piece is 8½ inches tall and has no pontil. It is not signed.

what is it? This important American pressed glass pattern has a number of names. The one most commonly used is "Three Face," but it is also called "Three Fates," "Three Graces," and "Three Sisters." The design was patented in 1878 by George Duncan and Sons of Pittsburgh, Pennsylvania, and it was the creation of their mold shop superintendent, John Ernest Miller.

Duncan originally called it the "#400" pattern, but "Three Face" was the alternate designation. No one knows for sure if the faces were modeled from a real person, but it has been speculated that Miller based them on the visage of his wife, Elizabeth.

These pieces always have frosted stems and bases supporting clear colorless glass vessels, and these vessels are almost always left plain and undecorated. The etched design on this one is most unusual, and it is in the "Huber" pattern.

It should also be mentioned that "Three Face" compotes came in a variety of sizes and styles. The covered high standard compote came in 8-, 9-, and 10-inch heights, and the low standard covered compote was 6 inches tall. The high standard open compote can be found in an 8½- to 9-inch size, and the low standard open compote is 6 inches tall.

"Three Face" has been widely reproduced, and collectors should be especially vigilant when buying the compote. The copies have been around for more than sixty years, but they lack the finely molded details of the original. Other "Three Face" pieces that have been reproduced include the sauce dish, the oil lamp, the champagne glass, the butter dish, both covered and open compotes, the sugar shaker, the biscuit or cracker jar, the creamer, and many other shapes. Any "Three Face" piece found in color is almost definitely a reproduction.

what is it worth? Original open compotes such as this one with no decoration on the bowl generally have an insurance replacement of around $300, but this one with the "Huber" decoration sold at auction in 2004 for $660.

item53

oval covered compote,
"Jumbo"

Valued at $9,625

8-inch-tall oval covered compote on a
high standard. The stem is hollow, and
the cover has a finial in the form of a
frosted elephant standing on a wheeled
platform. The piece is unsigned and in
good condition except for a small flake
on the platform that supports the
elephant figure and a chip on the inside
of the lid. The glass is clear colorless.

what is it?

This is a much beloved pattern of American pressed glass. It is called "Jumbo" and is a tribute to the famous elephant that is associated with P.T. Barnum's circus, "The Greatest Show on Earth."

The namesake "Jumbo" was an African elephant who is thought to have been born in the French Sudan in the late 1850s. He was captured in 1861 and sent to a zoo in Paris (the "Jardin des Plantes"), but a few years later, he was traded to the Royal Zoological Gardens in London Zoo for a rhinoceros.

In London, the elephant was named "Jumbo," which is thought to be a corruption of the Swahili word for "hello," which is "Jambo." The newly dubbed Jumbo grew to be 12 feet tall by the time of his death, but he was only about 11½ feet tall when he resided in London. While in London, Jumbo was used to give rides to children.

In the early 1880s, P.T. Barnum offered to buy Jumbo for $10,000, and Jumbo was sold and transported across the Atlantic, where he made his first appearance in Madison Square Garden in 1882. The receipts for that first performance were reportedly approximately $30,000.

Jumbo's career on this side of the Atlantic was fairly short lived because he was struck by a train in St. Thomas, Ontario, Canada, and died September 15, 1885. The death was a great financial loss to Barnum because Jumbo had become one of his major attractions. The resourceful entrepreneur called in a taxidermist to skin the ponderous pachyderm and remove the skeleton with the idea of creating two Jumbos—one made from the skin and the other a preserved skeleton.

The bones went to the Smithsonian Institution, and the stuffed hide traveled with the Barnum circus until 1889, when it was donated to Tufts University in Medford, Massachusetts. There it stayed until it was destroyed by fire in 1975 (it is said that the ashes are now kept in a peanut butter jar in a safe for good luck—but that may not be 100 percent true).

Jumbo captured the imagination of the American people, and both the Canton Glass Company and the Aetna Glass Company made "Jumbo"-pattern pressed glass in the mid-1880s (circa 1883). The piece pictured above is attributed to the Canton Glass Company, which was founded in Canton, Ohio, in 1883. It is said that it first produced a "Jumbo" pattern (originally called "Barker's White Elephant") in spring 1883. Canton burned to the ground in March 1890 and relocated to Marion, Indiana, in August of that year. The Aetna Glass Company was located in Bellaire, Ohio, and was in business from 1880 to 1889. Its "Jumbo" pieces with handles have what is said to be a portrait head of P.T. Barnum as a terminal for the handles (this pattern is sometimes called "Jumbo and Barnum").

Generally, "Jumbo" was made in clear colorless glass, and items in color are very uncommon. "Jumbo" can be found in a wide variety of table items including jam jars, castor sets, covered bowls, butter dishes, compotes with a more conical top and base than the one shown above and no wheels on the elephant's platform, and cups and saucers.

There are no recorded reproductions of this pattern.

what is it worth? At auction in 2003, this Canton Glass Company "Jumbo" compote sold for $9,625. Less rare "Jumbo" items sell for only a small fraction of that price. An example of this is the "Jumbo" creamer, which has an insurance replacement value of $450, and the "Jumbo and Barnum" covered sugar bowl, which has an insurance value of $500.

Related item

Set of three bottles in metal stand. Two of the bottles have shaker tops, and one has a lid that opens and has a cutout for the insertion of a spoon. The glass portion of the stand consists of three elephant heads with their curled up trunks as feet. The glass is transparent blue, and the piece is unsigned. It is in excellent condition except for an inner rim chip on the stand.

What is it?
This is the "Jumbo" castor set, and it consists of two shakers and a condiment or mustard jar that are all in a ribbed pattern. The lids are the originals.

What is it worth?
This set sold at auction in 2002 for $1,650.

item 54

butter dish, custard glass, "Louis XV"

what is it? This butter dish is a type of glass that most of today's collectors call "custard." The color of this ware can range from a vivid custard-like yellow to a rather pale and anemic yellow. Interesting, the name "custard" was not the name that this type of glass was given when it was first made.

This glass was initially produced in England by the Gates-Head-on-Tyne Glass Company located in Sowerby, which called it "Queen's Ivory Ware" when it started making the glass in the late 1870s. In the 1890s, American glass companies in the "Midwest" (mainly Pennsylvania and Ohio) started making this ware, and although some of the companies used the name "ivory," the designation "custard" began being applied to this type of opaque yellow glass, which can closely resemble egg custard.

The pattern found on this butter dish is known as "Louis XV" in honor of the French king of the same name, who ruled from 1715

Valued at $400

Two-piece butter dish that is approximately 7¾ inches in diameter and 7 inches tall. The glass is an opaque yellow with gold highlights that are significantly rubbed and has a raised design of chrysanthemums, leaves, and "C" scrolls. The piece sits on three feet and is unmarked.

to 1774. It was during Louis XV's reign that the French rococo style developed. It often featured curving asymmetrical ornamentation, and homage is paid to this type of design by the various "C" scrolls that are scattered here as accents to the gilded sprays of flowers and leaves.

This pattern was first made by the Northwood Glass Company of Indiana, Pennsylvania, in 1898, and in addition to the custard glass pictured above, "Louis XV" can be found in transparent emerald green. Northwood was founded by Englishman Harry Northwood in 1896, and the company went on to become one of the country's most important makers of high-quality pressed glass. Northwood is particularly known for its colored pressed glass and for its many fine patterns of carnival glass.

"Louis XV" came in a large table service that consisted of everything from salt shakers, spooners, and berry sets to tumblers, pitchers, and the rare toothpick holders. This pattern has been reproduced by the Imperial Glass Company of Bellaire, Ohio, and the Jeanette Glass Company of Jeanette, Pennsylvania. Fortunately, neither of these companies made it in custard glass.

Collectors should beware of any "Louis XV" pieces in a color other than custard or emerald green. All of the pieces in milk glass, ruby, pink, frosted crystal, and marbled slag are reproductions. These new pieces are also heavier than the older examples, and the raised parts are not as sharply molded.

what is it worth? Prices for "Louis XV" pieces can be rather modest, and this butter dish should be valued at $400.

Related item

7-inch-tall cruet with stopper with a body shaped like a sea shell. The glass is opaque yellow with gold highlights. It is signed "Northwood" on the bottom.

What is it?
This custard glass cruet is in the "Argonaut Shell" pattern, which, like "Louis XV," was made by the Northwood Glass Company of Indiana, Pennsylvania at the turn of the 20th century. In addition to custard, this pattern can be found in clear colorless, opalescent blue, and Vaseline.

It is most often found as the components of a water set (pitcher and tumblers) or berry set (large master berry bowl and smaller berry dishes), but covered butter dishes, creamers, sugar bowls, toothpick holders, salt and pepper shakers, and cruets can be found.

Reproductions are abundant in this pattern. The L.G. Wright Company of New Martinsville, West Virginia, started making "Argonaut Shell" in 1969. Many pieces are signed with an underlined "W" in a circle, but not all. In many cases, the custard glass is too pale (almost off-white), and the finial on the butter dish is a round knob rather than a well-defined shell shape. In addition, the gold on these later pieces is cold painted rather than fired on as it would have been on the originals.

What is it worth?
$900

item55

pitcher, chocolate glass, "Cactus"

Valued at $600

8-inch-tall water pitcher, opaque brown glass with tan highlights. It is decorated with a raised design that resembles cactus.

what is it?

"Chocolate" glass was first made in 1900, and it was the brainchild of Jacob Rosenthal at the Indiana Tumbler and Goblet Company of Greentown, Indiana. Collectors often shorthand the name of this company and refer to it as "Greentown" without saying the actual name of the company.

At one time, this type of glass was often called "chocolate slag," but that designation was dropped because many collectors got this ware confused with "caramel slag," which has something of the same color scheme except that "caramel slag" is more tan and creamy white than brown, is streakier, and can be a bit more translucent than true "chocolate" glass. Like "chocolate," "caramel slag" can be made into objects such as bowls and compotes, but unlike "chocolate," it is more often seen in lampshades and in decorative glass panels used in windows, outdoor architecture, and other types of ornamentation.

The Indiana Tumbler and Goblet Company was founded in February 1894 and remained in business until June 1903, when a disastrous fire burned the plant to the ground. The short-lived nature of this company means many of its products are quite rare, and many collectors are avidly interested in many of its products.

Chocolate glass can be found in a variety of patterns, including "Chrysanthemum Leaf," "Ruffled Eye," "Fleur-de-lis," "Dewey," "Running Deer," "Geneva," "Cattail and Water Lily," and "Orange Tree," among many others. Chocolate glass has been reproduced, and the "Cactus" pattern was reissued starting in 1959 by the Fenton Art Glass Company of Williamstown, West Virginia.

Fenton's "Cactus" was made for the Levay Distributing Company of Edwardsville, Illinois. Besides chocolate, it was made in a variety of colors, including blue opalescent, topaz opalescent, Colonial Amber, Colonial Blue, Colonial Pink, milk glass, Red Sunset carnival, Aqua Opal carnival, and Custard Satin. This line was made for quite a long time, and after 1967, Fenton called the pattern, "Desert Tree."

Only five of the Fenton "Cactus" pieces are reproductions of old forms; these are the cracker jar, the creamer, the sugar bowl, the bonbon dish, and the shakers. The pitcher seen above was not reproduced by Fenton in chocolate.

what is it worth?

The water pitcher on page 137 should be valued at $600.

Mug in opaque glass that is brown mottled with tan. The piece is 5 inches tall and features the raised image of men drinking outdoors.

What is it?

This chocolate glass mug in Greentown's "Outdoor Drinking Scene" pattern should not be confused with the pieces that have an indoor drinking scene or ones that show a troubadour, known as "Serenade." These mugs can also be found in a larger 8½-inch-tall size that has a pouring lip.

What is it worth?

$450

butter dish, "Holly Amber"

Valued at $2,100

Two-part butter dish with mottled color that ranges from a transparent amber to an opalescent creamy white. The piece is decorated with panels of holly berries and leaves between beaded borders. The top is highly domed, and the bottom is flat with a deeply scalloped edge. It is unsigned.

what is it? This is another pressed glass product of the Indiana Tumbler and Goblet Company of Greentown, Indiana (generally just called "Greentown"). The glass itself should be called "Golden Agate," and the pattern is "Holly." Originally, Greentown just called the line "number 450," but modern collectors refer to the examples with the "Golden Agate" color and the "Holly" pattern as "Holly Amber," which is actually a misnomer.

This type of glass was made for only a brief period—between January 1, 1903, and June 13, 1903, which was the day the factory burned down. Like chocolate glass, which was discussed earlier, "Holly Amber" was the creation of Jacob Rosenthal, who went to Fenton after the tragic fire at Greentown. Because of its limited time of production, this glass is exceedingly rare, and can be very expensive.

Actually, the "Holly" pattern was designed by Frank Jackson, and it can be found in both chocolate glass and what is called "Holly Blue." Both of these alternative colors are extremely hard to find.

Holly Amber can be found in an extensive table setting, including a jelly compote, covered compote, cake stand, creamer, mustard pot, pickle dish, cruet, pitcher, spooner, syrup pitcher, toothpick holder, sauce dish, tray, tumbler, mug, parfait, salt and pepper shakers, and vase.

"Holly Amber" has been widely reproduced, and the fakes far outnumber the originals. The contemporary pieces were all made from new molds, and the mold work is not as good as it was on the originals. This can be seen in the beading (which can be too large or too small) and in the holly stems, which are too thick. In addition, reproduction pieces tend to have a single holly berry with a leaf on either side of the stem, while the originals have a single berry as well as clusters of two or three berries. Reproductions are heavier and thicker than the originals as a general rule.

what is it worth? Greentown made two types of butter dishes. This one has a flat bottom, but there was another that had a low pedestal foot. The example pictured above should be valued at $2,100. The pedestal foot variety is worth approximately twice that amount.

3½-inch-tall tumbler with beaded rim. The glass had mottled colors that range from a translucent amber to a creamy opalescent white. The decoration is panels with holly leaves and berries interspersed with plain opalescent panels. There are two very small chips, one on the rim and one on the base.

What is it?

In collecting, little details can mean a lot. In this case, this Greentown tumbler has a beaded rim, and this is a form of "Holly Amber" (or "Golden Agate," as it is more properly called) that is very rare.

What is it worth?

The two tiny flakes on this piece are not aesthetically off-putting, and it sold at auction in early 2005 for an astounding $7,810.

item 57

spooner, "Single Vine Bellflower"

Valued at $9,900

Spooner, 5⅝ inches tall, decorated
with a pattern of flowers, leaves, and
a vine against a finely ribbed
background. The glass is a very pleasing
shade of transparent cobalt blue. The
piece is unsigned.

what is it? The piece on page 143 is most commonly called "Single Vine Bellflower," but it is also known as "Ribbed Leaf." There is also a "Double Vine Bellflower" pattern that is much the same as the pattern above, but it has double entwining vines.

"Bellflower" came with a variety of base designs. This one has forty-five rays on the bottom, but examples can be found with rays that fan out from the center to the edge of the foot, rays that fan out from the center but terminate in a ring short of the edge of the foot, and rays that are arranged in a wide band around the outside of the foot—just to name a few.

The ribbing on "Bellflower" can vary greatly, with some pieces having very fine ribbing and others having coarse ribbing (sometimes, pieces are classified as "single vine–fine rib, single vine–coarse rib, double vine–fine rib, and double vine–coarse rib). It should be mentioned that although most of the "Bellflower" that is encountered is pressed, some of it was blown into a mold and has a pontil as a telltale sign.

Bellflower was first made by the Boston and Sandwich Glass Company sometime just before 1840, but it was also made by several other companies, notably McKee and Brothers of Pittsburgh, Pennsylvania. The example pictured above is thought to be from the third quarter of the nineteenth century (i.e., 1850–1875). Bellflower is most commonly found in clear colorless, but it was also made very rarely in colors such as amber, opalescent, green, milk glass, and a range of blues—opaque, sapphire, and cobalt.

Reproductions of single vine–fine rib "Bellflower" were made as early as the late 1930s but this early reproduction was made only as a tumbler, and has a greenish-yellow color that is the giveaway that it is not an original.

In addition, "Bellflower" has been reproduced by the Metropolitan Museum of Art in New York and the Smithsonian Institution in Washington, D.C. Both of these are clearly marked on the bases with "MMA" for the Metropolitan and "SI" for the Smithsonian.

what is it worth? This spooner, which (as the name implies) is a vessel for holding spoons, is in a very rare color, and sold at auction in 2004 for $9,900.

item58

table setting, "Monkey"

Valued at $3,900

Four-piece table setting consisting of a two-piece covered butter dish, a cream pitcher, a spoon holder, and a covered sugar bowl. The glass is fiery opalescent with raised designs of monkeys. The butter dish is 6 inches tall and 7¼ inches in diameter, the creamer is 5¾ inches tall, the spooner is 5 inches high, and the covered sugar bowl is 7½ inches tall. The creamer is badly damaged with a crack starting at the base of the handle, and there is a small chip on the under edge of the butter lid.

a. two-piece covered butter dish
b. spoon holder
c. covered sugar bowl
d. cream pitcher

what is it? There are several American pressed glass patterns that feature animals. These include deer and stags, giraffes, elephants, lions, squirrels, beavers, hunting dogs, polar bears, and kittens—but one of the more charming of these patterns features monkeys sitting under trees.

"Monkey" is thought to be a product of the early third quarter of the nineteenth century, but there is some disagreement about the original manufacturer. In the past, it has been attributed to George Duncan and Sons of Pittsburgh, but more modern research has suggested that this pattern may have been a product of the Valley Glass Company in Beaver Falls, Pennsylvania.

These pieces are most commonly found in clear colorless glass, but white opalescent pieces and examples that are decorated with unfired-on colors or an amber stain have been found. "Monkey" was made in a number of forms, and besides the pieces shown above, it can be found on such items as tumblers, mugs, pickle jars, jam jars, and celery vases. Interestingly, no "Monkey"-pattern goblets were made in the original production.

"Monkey" has been reproduced, but the quality and detail of the reproductions fall far short of the originals. The new pieces were reportedly made in Korea and lack detail in the monkeys' fur and on the tree bark. There is also less detailing on the monkeys' feet and hands, and the images tend to be a bit blurry.

what is it worth? Finding a four-piece table set in "Monkey" like this one is very difficult, and even with the damage, this set sold at auction in 2000 for $3,900.

item 59

sugar bowl, "Log Cabin"

Valued at $2,100

6½-inch-tall rectangular covered boxlike vessel shaped like a log cabin complete with door, windows, and chimney. The glass is in transparent blue, and there are a few flakes under the rim and on the base that do not affect the aesthetics.

what is it? This pattern is a celebration of America's pioneer past. All of the pieces in this series appear to be made from logs and are rectangular in shape. The standards used on the compotes are shaped like tree trunks, but the rest of the items in this grouping stand on four small log feet.

The line is known as "Log Cabin," and all the pieces except the sauce dish and the covered butter dish have windows and doors, and the doors are always depicted with a latch. "Log Cabin" was an 1870 product of the Central Glass Company of Wheeling, West Virginia. When it was first made, "Log Cabin" was referred to as Central's pattern number 748.

The Central Glass Company was founded in Wheeling in 1863 but did not adopt a charter under this name until 1867. In 1891, it became "Factory O" of the United States Glass Company but pulled away from this amalgamation in 1896 and renamed itself the Central Glass Works. The Great Depression almost put it out of business for good, and it did close in 1930 only to reopen in 1933. It closed forever in 1939, and the Imperial Glass Company bought its molds.

"Log Cabin" is generally found in clear colorless glass, but examples in amber, blue, and Vaseline turn up from time to time and are considered to be rare. Reproductions in this pattern have been made, and the covered sugar bowl is one of them. Other reproduced forms are the creamer, the spooner, and a cough drop dispenser with an advertising logo on it. To distinguish the difference between new and old "Log Cabin" pieces, look for the latch on the door—on the new items, this feature will be missing.

what is it worth? Some "Log Cabin" items in clear colorless glass should be valued for insurance purposes for less than $200, but this blue sugar bowl sold at auction in 2002 for $2,100.

item 60

water pitcher, "Memphis"

Valued at $400

8¾-inch-tall water pitcher with the appearance of cut glass. Green transparent glass with heavy gilding.

what is it? There are many patterns of pressed glass that have the names of states: "Alabama," "Colorado," "Texas," "California," "Dakota," "New Hampshire," "Pennsylvania," and "Maryland" to name just a few.

Far fewer pressed glass patterns have city names in them; these include "Venice," "Palm Beach," "Kokomo," "Manhattan," and "Tokyo." Perhaps the most famous of the patterns with a city name is "Memphis," which is also known as "Doll's Eye." Why this particular pattern has an alternate name is apparent in the piece pictured above, which has the eye-shaped portion of its pattern clearly highlighted in gold.

"Memphis" was a product of the Northwood Glass Company, which originally designated it pattern number 19. Harry Northwood founded his company in Indiana, Pennsylvania, in 1896, and in 1899, he became part of the National Glass Company. By 1901, Northwood was unhappy with this situation, and he broke away from National.

In 1902, he purchased the old Hobbs, Brockunier plant in Wheeling, West Virginia, and began operating this plant and his original facility in Indiana, Pennsylvania. In 1904, Northwood leased the

latter plant to Thomas Dugan and W.G. Minnemeyer and began operating only the facility in Wheeling.

In 1908, Northwood decided to start making carnival glass, and it is at about this time that the "Memphis" pattern was first made. "Memphis" can be found in a wide variety of colors, including clear colorless and the green seen above, and in carnival, it was made in marigold, amethyst, cobalt blue, white, ice blue, and others.

There are no recorded reproductions of this pattern.

what is it worth? When it comes to the value of a piece of "Memphis," color and type of surface finish are everything. Take, for example, a "Memphis" punch bowl and base. In carnival glass, this piece is worth about $500 in marigold, $600 in amethyst, and $700 in green, but in ice blue, the value jumps to around $6,000. The green pitcher above, which is not carnival glass, is worth $400.

Related item

3½-inch-tall creamer-sized pitcher. The body of the creamer is essentially square and is made from frosted clear colorless glass that is accented with a cross that has been stained gold or amber.

What is it?

This pattern has a number of names. Collectors commonly call this "Klondike," but its original name was Dalzell's No. 75 (Dalzell's No. 75D is the same pattern without the gold or amber stain). Pieces in this pattern are also known as "Amberette," "Alaska," and "English Hobnail Cross."

Although previously attributed to Hobbs, Brockunier of Wheeling, West Virginia, and A.J. Beatty Company of Steubenville, Ohio, it is now known that this pattern was a product of Dalzell, Gilmore & Leighton in Findlay, Ohio. Pieces can be found in clear colorless glass, satin-finished clear colorless glass, clear colorless with a satin finish and amber stain on the cross decoration, and a lilac-colored stain on the cross. This last variation is extremely rare.

Some sources say "Klondike" or "Amberette" was made as early as 1888, but most references say it originated in 1898. This is a very popular but hard-to-find pattern, and it can be rather valuable.

Reproductions of "Klondike" have been reported, but not the creamer.

What is it worth?

$350

item61

water pitcher, "Cabbage Leaf"

Valued at $1,250

Water pitcher that is 10¼ inches tall.
The glass is transparent and
frosted amber with the lower portion
of the vessel resembling frosted
cabbage leaves.

what is it?

This pressed glass pattern is appropriately called "Cabbage Leaf" or "Frosted Cabbage Leaf," and it is most often found in clear colorless glass. Occasionally, however, examples in blue or amber will turn up, but these are considered to be uncommon.

Until fairly recently, no one knew who made this pattern, but now it is known that this was pattern number 135 of the Riverside Glass Works of Wellsburg, West Virginia. The company was in business from 1879 to 1907, and this pattern is thought to be from the very late 1870s or early 1880s.

This design came in a very limited number of pieces, and the covered pieces that were made have finials in the shape of a rabbit's head. Known shapes include a rabbit plate, a compote, a leaf-shaped relish or pickle dish, an egg cup, a covered cheese dish, a cake stand, a cup, and a celery vase.

The combination of the cabbage leaves and the rabbit heads brings to mind the children's story of "Peter Cottontail," and these pieces are very charming and desirable to collectors of pressed glass. Unfortunately, this pattern is so charming and appealing that it has been widely reproduced, and the vast majority of all pieces seen on the current antiques market are relatively modern.

The first reproductions of "Cabbage Leaf" appeared in the 1960s and were a product of the L.G. Wright Glass Company of New Martinsville, West Virginia. These first pieces were reportedly a 5-inch wine goblet and a 6-inch water goblet that were made in the three old colors—clear colorless, blue, and amber. It should be noted that there are no old "Cabbage Leaf" goblets (it was not one of the original forms made), and any goblet that is encountered is a modern fake.

In addition to the goblets, L.G. Wright made "Cabbage Leaf" butter dishes, celery vases, covered compotes, creamers, pitchers, rabbit plates, sauce dishes, spooners, and sugar bowls. Most reproductions are rather heavy and poorly molded, with veining on the leaves that is too faint and not realistic.

what is it worth?

To date, this pitcher has not been reproduced, but it is hard to price because old "Cabbage Leaf" pieces in amber do not come onto the market very often. However, after checking with Karen Reed of Green Valley Auction Company, which is one of the country's most prestigious sellers of antique glass, the price of this piece should be $1,250.

Valued at $175

9-inch-tall vase-like piece in clear
colorless glass with a raised design
taken from the Gilbert and Sullivan
operetta "H.M.S. Pinafore."

what is it? This vessel, called a "celery vase," was designed to hold bunches of celery at the dinner table. The pattern name is not quite so simple because collectors call this by a wide variety of designations. The most common is "Actress," but "Theatrical," "Pinafore," "Annie," and "Jenny Lind" are sometimes used.

The pieces feature portraits of famous actresses of the late nineteenth century as well as actors performing in plays. The cake stand, for example, has Annie Pixley and Maude Grainger, while the covered cheese dish has Sanderson Moffitt as "The Lone Fisherman" on the cover and Stuart Robson and William Crane as the "Two Dromios" on the base. The water pitcher has a scene from "Romeo and Juliet," and the goblet depicts Kate Claxton and Lotta Crabtree. The smaller bread plate, the mug, the milk pitcher, and the spooner all show a scene from "H.M.S. Pinafore."

The celery vase pictured above came in two varieties—one decorated with the depiction of an actress's head and the other featuring a scene from "H.M.S. Pinafore." Of the two, the style with the "H.M.S. Pinafore" is on a pedestal and is a bit more valuable than the one with just the actress's head.

Celery vases, or "celery glasses" as they are often called in England, were first made in Great Britain in the late eighteenth century, and they were designed to hold stalks of celery in the upright position. At that time, celery was something of an exotic vegetable, and it was served at the table in these special containers. By the end of the nineteenth century, celery vases were out of fashion and no longer made.

The manufacturer of these pieces was Adams and Company of Pittsburgh, Pennsylvania, and they were first made circa 1880. Some sources list the LaBelle Glass Company and the Crystal Glass Company, both of Bridgeport, Ohio, as the makers, but recent information has proven this to be incorrect. This pattern was made only in clear or clear and frosted with the clear pieces being a little less valuable than the frosted ones.

There is only one known reproduction of a piece in the "Actress" line, and this is the pickle dish, which has "Love's Request is Pickles" embossed on the outside base. This was first produced in 1957 by the Imperial Glass Company and came in a variety of colors. These should present no problems for collectors because they are marked with the Imperial "I G" monogram (the "G" is superimposed over the "I"). In addition, "Actress" was never made in colors, and any piece found in some color other than clear colorless or clear colorless with frosting is a reproduction.

what is it worth? This is a fascinating and unusual pattern, and one might think that pieces in this line are rather valuable, but for the most part, they are not. The 6 1/2-inch-tall milk pitcher with the "H.M.S. Pinafore" design is the most expensive of the pieces with this specific design and is worth $350. The celery vase pictured above is valued at $175.

item 63

water pitcher, "Wading Heron"

Valued at $350

9-inch-tall straight-sided
water pitcher with a scalloped
edge around the top. The glass is
transparent green with a raised
decoration of a bird wading
among bull rushes.

what is it? There are a number of pressed glass patterns
that feature the image of a long-legged bird. One seems to be
catching a snake in his bill, another seems to be devouring a
snake while looking at the moon, and another has a frosted bird
in a wetland. These birds are variously identified as a heron, a
stork, a crane, a flamingo, or, oddly in one case, an ostrich.

The bird on the pitcher above is a heron, and the pattern is called
"Wading Heron." It was a product of the U.S. Glass Company,
which was an amalgamation of eighteen formerly independent
glass companies. It was an attempt to survive during hard times,
and it was founded July 1, 1891.

The various factories in this grouping were given names that were
letters of the alphabet. The Bryce Brothers of Pittsburgh, Pennsyl-

vania, for example, were designated "Factory B," and Tiffin Glass of Tiffin, Ohio, became "Factory R." No one seems to know exactly which factory of the U.S. Glass Company made the "Wading Heron" pattern, but the design is generally given a circa 1900 date (one source says 1915, but that is too late).

This pattern can be found in clear colorless and in green. Reproductions are not known to exist.

what is it worth? The green color of this piece is considered to be rare, and this pitcher is worth $350.

item 64

water pitcher, "Old Oaken Bucket"

Valued at $250

8¼-inch-tall water pitcher in the form
of an oaken bucket with bail handle. The
glass is transparent amethyst.

what is it? Like so many pressed glass patterns, this one goes by several similar names. One is "Wooden Bucket," and another is "Wooden Pail," but we like "Oaken Bucket" (or "Old Oaken Bucket") a bit better. This pattern was made by Bryce Brothers of Pittsburgh, Pennsylvania, circa 1882, by Bryce, Higbee and Company, also of Pittsburgh, in the 1880s, and by the U.S. Glass Company after 1891, when Bryce Brothers became that company's Factory "B."

Bryce Brothers is not a company that springs readily to the mind of many collectors of American pressed glass, but it has a long and distinguished history that began in 1850 and, according to one source, ended in 1965. Recounting the details of the long and convoluted history of this company can be confusing and not necessary to a discussion of its "Old Oaken Bucket" pieces, which were made in a variety of shapes and sizes.

Some of the more fascinating of these pieces are the jelly containers, which came in ⅓-pint, half-pint, and quart sizes. They had tin lids with "The Old Oaken Bucket" embossed on them and a real bail handle that was not just molded into the glass. This pattern was also made in toothpick holders, ice buckets, open and covered sugar bowls, creamers, spooners, and water pitchers, such as the one pictured at left.

Interestingly, this pattern was made as a "toy" set, or a small-size set that was meant to be used by children. Pieces of "Old Oaken Bucket" can be found in shades of blue, clear colorless, amber, yellow (variously listed as canary or Vaseline), and, very rarely, amethyst. The jelly containers can also be found in marigold-colored carnival glass.

No reproductions are reported for this pattern.

what is it worth? $250

item65

carnival glass bowl, "Dugan Cherry"

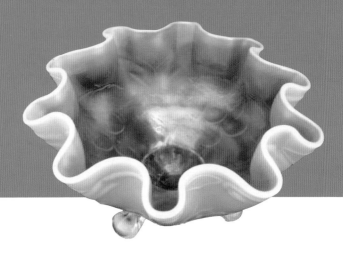

what is it? Carnival glass was first made in the United States around 1905, and it is said to have been an attempt to imitate the iridescent surfaces on glassware that were being made by Tiffany and others. Under the iridescent surfaces, carnival glass was made with a rainbow of colored glass that included amethyst, marigold (a kind of bright golden amber), several shades of blue, several shades of green, white, red, smoke (grayish transparent glass the color of smoke), and many other colors that show up from time to time.

The color of the piece pictured above is called "peach opalescent," and it is marigold with the addition of white opalescence. Carnival can be found in a number of these opalescent colors, including ice blue opalescent (called "aqua opalescent"), ice green opalescent, amethyst opalescent, lime green opalescent, red opalescent, and Vaseline opalescent. The opalescent ice colors (blue and green) are often the rarest and most valuable of these shades.

The pattern on this particular piece pictured is known as "Cherry" or more precisely "Dugan Cherry." This latter specification is nec-

Valued at $475

Three-footed, ruffled edge bowl that is 8½ inches in diameter. The glass is iridescent and is in shades of peach and white. The pattern is raised cherries, stems, and leaves. The piece is unmarked.

essary because there are a number of other carnival patterns that featured the representation of cherries, and they include "Cherry" by Millersburg, "Cherry and Cable" by Northwood, "Cherry Chain" by Fenton, "Cherry Circles" by Fenton, and "Cherry/Hobnail" by Millersburg.

As was mentioned earlier, the Dugan Glass Company operated the old Northwood plant in Indiana, Pennsylvania, after Northwood shifted his entire operation to the old Hobbs, Brockunier plant in Wheeling, West Virginia, in 1904. In 1913, the name of the company was changed to the Diamond Glass Company, and the trademark of a "D" inside a diamond was adopted. Diamond/Dugan closed in 1931 when the facility was destroyed by fire.

This footed bowl was made circa 1910, and there are no known reproductions.

what is it worth? There were two bowls made in "Dugan Cherry." One is flat and 8 inches in diameter, and the other is footed and 8½ inches in diameter. The flat pieces are much less valuable than the footed examples, and one in marigold is worth only about $70, while one in amethyst should be valued at only about $5 to $10 more. In peach opalescent, the flat bowls are worth about $225. In contrast, a marigold footed bowl is worth $250, one in amethyst is worth $425, and one in peach opalescent like the one pictured above is worth $475.

Related items

1 Tumbler, 4 inches tall with the raised image of a large flower blossom. The color is amethyst, and the piece is unsigned.

What is it?
This attractive pattern is called "Dahlia," and it is a product of the Dugan Glass Company of Indiana, Pennsylvania. This is a very uncommon pattern that was made in only a few shapes. It can be found in a water set consisting of a pitcher and tumblers, a creamer (or spooner) and sugar bowl, a butter dish, and two sizes of footed bowls.

It can be found in marigold or amethyst and more rarely in white. The glass Dugan used to make the "Dahlia" pieces is very high quality, and the iridescence is unusually good. Both the pitcher and the tumbler are considered to be rare, and assembling a full water set is difficult.

What is it worth?
$200

2 Ruffled edge bowl with a heavily embossed inside pattern consisting of a central butterfly surrounded by tulips and leaves. On the exterior, there is an embossed feather scroll design. The bowl is footed and 13 inches in diameter. The color of the glass is amethyst.

What is it?
This Dugan pattern is appropriately called "Butterfly and Tulip," and it was made by the Dugan Glass Company. This pattern is known only in bowl forms, and it is found only in amethyst or marigold.

What is it worth?
In early 2005, this bowl sold at auction for $2,090.

item66

carnival glass bowls, "Peacock and Urn"

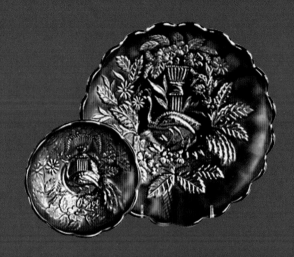

Valued at $1,550

Five bowls, one 10¼ inches in diameter
and four that are 5½ inches in diameter.
The glass is amethyst in color and has a
raised design of a peacock standing in
front of an urn on a pedestal. This
central image is surrounded with leaves
and small flowers. The underside of each
piece is signed with an underlined "N"
inside a circle.

The Northwood mark most often found.

what is it? This pattern is known to collectors as "Peacock and Urn," and it was made in several variations by three different companies—Fenton, Northwood, and Millersburg. The Fenton and the various Millersburg versions are all unsigned, but the Northwood examples all carry the characteristic underlined "N" in a circle mark.

Distinguishing the unmarked Millersburg "Peacock and Urn" pieces from the unmarked Fenton examples is easy because the Fenton pieces have an exterior pattern known as "Bearded Berry" that Millersburg specimens do not have. The Northwood and the Millersburg patterns are very similar, but the Northwood pieces are almost always signed.

Northwood was founded in 1896 in Indiana, Pennsylvania, by Harry Northwood, but the company did not produce carnival glass until after the firm had moved to the old Hobbs, Brockunier facility in Wheeling, West Virginia. The first Northwood carnival was marketed in 1908, and it was perhaps the company's most popular product for the next ten years. By the time of Northwood's death in 1919, however, the demand for this type of glass had diminished and production had slowed to a trickle.

Northwood's "Peacock and Urn" pattern was made in a very limited number of pieces, and these include a berry set, an ice cream set, and two plates—a 6-inch-diameter size and an 11-inch-diameter size—both of which are very rare. This pattern is found in a variety of colors, including the standard shades of marigold, amethyst, green, and blue, but it can be found in aqua opalescent, ice blue, and white as well.

The exact function of the pieces pictured above is open to some conjecture because the diameter of the bowl ($10^{1}/_{4}$ inches) suggests that it was originally intended to be used to serve ice cream because the master berry bowl is a bit smaller at 9 inches in diameter. The smaller bowls are where the problem arises because the individual berry bowls are reportedly 5 inches in diameter, and the individual ice cream dishes are supposedly 6 inches in diameter.

The individual serving bowls pictured above are $5^{1}/_{2}$ inches in diameter, which puts them between the two sizes. This may be a measuring problem or it may be an unusual size, but these are probably berry bowls, which are a bit more valuable than the individual ice cream bowls.

what is it worth?

In June 2002, this set sold at auction for $1,550, which is its approximate insurance replacement value if the set is composed of the master ice cream bowl and four individual berry bowls. (Note: Color in carnival glass can be extremely important; a master ice cream bowl like the one above, but in aqua opalescent, should be valued for insurance purposes at approximately $32,000 or perhaps a bit more.)

Related item

8½-inch diameter bowl, iridized blue color with a raised design of a horseshoe and riding crop with the phrase "Good Luck" above. This central motif is surrounded by a wreath of flowers, berries, stalks of wheat, stems, and leaves. The piece is unmarked.

What is it?
Known as the "Good Luck" pattern, this piece is a product of the Northwood Glass Company. It can be found on bowls and plates and came in a wide variety of colors, including marigold, blue, amethyst, green, ice blue, sapphire blue, and aqua opalescent. In its day, it must have been a very popular gift item that was given for all sorts of special occasions.

There are a number of variations in this pattern. One has an exterior "basketweave" design with fewer flowers, leaves, berries, and stalks of wheat in the wreath, while others have stippling (shallow dots) on the surface. The presence of this stippling can raise the value of a "Good Luck" piece by 20 to 30 percent.

What is it worth?
In blue, the value of this bowl is $450, but in marigold it is $250, and in aqua opalescent it jumps to $2,000.

item 67

carnival glass bowl, "Dragon and Lotus"

Valued at $4,300

9-inch-diameter bowl, red iridized glass with a raised decoration of dragons and flower blossoms that resemble roses. The piece has a flat base and is unsigned.

what is it? Despite the fact that the flowers look like roses, this pattern made by the Fenton Art Glass Company of Williamstown, West Virginia, is called "Dragon and Lotus." This is one of the more popular of the Fenton patterns, and it can be found in a rainbow of colors, including the standard marigold, green, blue, and amethyst, plus peach opalescent, iridized milk glass, aqua opalescent, Vaseline opalescent, amber, smoke, and red.

This pattern can be found on two types of 9-inch-diameter bowls (flat and footed), a nut dish, and a 9½-inch-diameter plate. Of these shapes, the plate is extremely rare, with prices between $1,500 and $10,000 depending on the color, with the least expensive being peach opalescent and the most expensive being red. In fact, red is one of the most desirable of the carnival glass colors, and it is very hard to find on pieces made during the early part of the twentieth century.

Fenton started making carnival glass in about 1908 and continues to make it to this day. Fenton was a very prolific maker of this type of glass, and it is said that over the years, it made between 130 and 150 different patterns in this type of glass.

what is it worth? In the "Dragon and Lotus" pattern, red is the rarest and most desired color. The flat compote pictured above is worth $4,300, while the footed one is worth just a bit less at $4,000.

item 68

carnival glass bowl, "Big Fish"

Valued at $1,050

Iridized green glass bowl with the raised image of a very realistic fish swimming among flowering aquatic plants. The bowl is 8 inches in diameter and has a scalloped edge.

what is it? In 1908, John Fenton sold his interest in the Fenton Art Glass Company and began building his own glass factory in Millersburg, Ohio. The Millersburg Glass Company opened in 1909, and the first molds were designed by Fenton himself.

The first glass made was very high-quality clear colorless glass, but iridized carnival glass in shades of amethyst, green, and marigold went into production shortly thereafter. In 1910, Millersburg introduced a new finish to its iridized glassware called the "radium" finish, which is distinguished by its mirror-like quality.

This new surface was very distinctive, but it did not take long for other glass makers such as the Imperial Glass Company to imitate it with some degree of success. Initially, the Millersburg Glass Company prospered, but by 1911, bankruptcy loomed, and the company was renamed the "Radium Glass Company."

There was an attempt to save the factory, but it failed and the company was sold to the Jefferson Glass Company in 1913. Millersburg glass can be difficult to find because of the short-lived nature of the company, and many of its patterns are quite rare. Beyond the rarity factor, collectors are attracted to Millersburg glass because of its high quality and because it is some of the most beautiful and interesting carnival glass made.

The Millersburg pattern pictured at left is called "Big Fish" and was made in a variety of bowl forms. There was, for example, a rose bowl, a square bowl, a tri-cornered bowl, a banana bowl (or boat), and this round bowl. They were made in shades of marigold, amethyst, green, and Vaseline—with Vaseline being the rarest color.

what is it worth? In 2003, this bowl sold at auction for $1,050. A similar example in Vaseline would be at least six times that valuable.

item 69

box, "Wave Crest"

Valued at $600

5¼-inch-diameter box decorated with hand-painted ferns on opaque white glass. The interior has the remnants of the original satin lining. The two pieces of glass are held together by hinged metal collars, and there is a simple closure on the front. On the bottom, there is a small circular paper label that reads "Wave Crest Ware patented October ..." (remainder is unreadable).

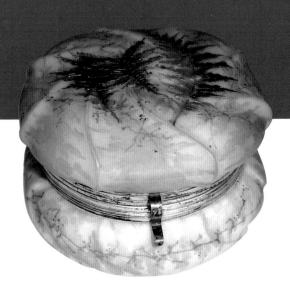

what is it? Wave Crest is a product of the C.F. Monroe Company of Meriden, Connecticut, and was patented October 4, 1892. Charles Fabian Monroe started his career in the glass industry as a designer, but he made his mark as a decorator. He taught china and glass decorating classes and ran what were called "Art Rooms" on Main Street in Meriden while he was otherwise employed by the Meriden Flint Glass Company. In his "Art Rooms," he sold paintings, cut glass pieces made by his employer, artist supplies, various kinds of bric-a-brac, and items such as tiles and lampshades that he had decorated in his studio in the rear of the building.

Example of a C.F. Monroe "Wave Crest" mark.

Another mark found on C.F. Monroe's "Wave Crest."

The "Art Rooms" closed in 1885, but Monroe continued selling the art supplies and teaching glass decorating to the public. He founded the C.F. Monroe Company in 1892, the same year in which the production of his Wave Crest ware began. The C.F. Monroe Company did not manufacture its own glass but bought blanks (i.e. undecorated pieces of glass or china) from other companies such as Pairpoint (formerly Mt. Washington), some French companies, and reportedly, from the Roedifer Glass Company of Bel Air, Ohio.

There is no evidence that Wave Crest was ever made using blown or blown-in-mold blanks. Instead, it was always made using pressed opal glass, which is a translucent (but almost opaque) white glass with a bit of fire like the opal gem, or very rarely, on crystal. The "blanks" that the company bought were decorated by several talented artists including Carl V. Helmschmeid, who created a shape that the company patented. This box pictured above is in that shape, which is called "Helmschmeid Swirl."

The process of making Wave Crest often began with giving the blank a "bath" in acid, which gave the surface a satin finish. Not all pieces were given this satin finish; some were left glossy. Almost all of the crystal pieces were given a satin bath, but a few glossy examples are known.

It should be noted that the crystal pieces are generally found enamel stained in shades of blue, pink, and clear colorless, and although these pieces are often called "crystal Wave Crest," most collectors do not feel that they belong in this category. The shapes are often the same, but true Wave Crest should always be on an opal glass blank.

On the opal pieces, a background color was added next. These were usually a light, almost transparent pastel treatment in matte colors of blue, pink, yellow, or ivory. Other colors used include sage green, royal blue, rose, and even purple and black. Sometimes, the colors were very dark—an almost chocolate brown, a brick red, or a glossy dark green. Sometimes, the areas that were to be painted were left pure white to make the design more dramatic.

The typical decoration found on Wave Crest is floral, and this category includes the ferns that were used so often. Rarer subject matter includes portraits of nude and clothed women, children, birds, animals, landscapes, seascapes, and scenic depictions with human figures. Transfer prints were used on Wave Crest, but many of these pieces are not as highly desired as some of the hand painted items unless the transfer print is very unusual, such as one that has the image of a Native American chief in full headdress.

Typically, collectors find Wave Crest boxes in an astonishing variety of sizes and shapes that range from the tiny to the huge, but C.F. Monroe also made vases, wall plaques, humidors, wall-mounted whisk broom holders, ferneries, salt and pepper shakers, biscuit jars, match holders, ewers, spittoons, cream pitchers, sugar bowls, card holders, hair receivers, ashtrays, bill spikes, rocker blotters, clocks, and ink wells, among others.

Wave Crest pieces are often marked, but not always. In the case of the piece pictured here, it is marked with a paper label, and it is a miracle that this has survived largely intact for approximately a hundred years. As with most glass, antique enthusiasts need to learn to recognize Wave Crest on sight and not rely on marks.

In addition to its decorated opal ware, C.F. Monroe made some fine cut glass in the American Brilliant Period style. Unfortunately, the demand for hand-painted (and transfer decorated) opal glass items died in approximately 1910, and C.F. Monroe went out of business in 1916.

Reproductions of Wave Crest are not a problem, but other companies did make similar wares, and these are (for the most part) less desirable to many current collectors.

what is it worth? This is a rather common piece of Wave Crest. The shape is typical and so is the decoration. Still, it is lovely and in good condition and should be valued at $600.

C. F. M. CO. NAKARA

One of the marks associated with C.F. Monroe's Nakara ware.

1 Vase with gilded metal mountings in the rococo manner. The vase is 17½ inches tall overall, and the glass portion is 12 inches tall. The base glass is opal, and the decoration depicts sailing ships in a harbor. It is signed "Nakara" and "C. F. M. CO."

What is it?

"Nakara" is the third trade name used by the C.F. Monroe Company of Meriden, Connecticut, on its decorated opal wares. Like "Kelva," it is rarer than standard "Wave Crest." "Nakara" is most often distinguished by its deep background colors, which are enhanced with beading and rococo-style scrolls. "Nakara" generally has an acid finish, but glossy-finished items are known to exist.

"Nakara" is often found with very elaborate decorations of such things as "Gibson Girls" and other portraits and scenes—both landscapes and seascapes. Many of these were applied with transfer prints, but completely hand-painted examples are also known.

The shape and metalwork on this vase appeared in C.F. Monroe's 1901 catalog. With a full-length portrait for decoration, it was listed as style number 278-RY. The entry was listed as "Opal Vases, Elaborately Decorated and Artistically Mounted With Richly Gold-Plated Trimmings."

What is it worth?

This piece was not inexpensive when it was made at the turn of the twentieth century, and it is far from inexpensive today. In 2003, it sold at auction for $10,500.

2 Jardinière, 6¾-inch diameter at top rim with a raised foot. The piece is straight sided and has a decoration of a Venetian scene with a gondola on a canal with a bridge and houses on one side and boats on the other. This piece has a gilt ring above the decoration and a little roughness to the rim. It is unsigned.

What is it?
Serious antiques enthusiasts have to have reference books to identify and pursue the objects they want to collect. Unsigned, this piece might be overlooked as just another piece of white glass. A good reference book on C.F. Monroe, however, will reveal that this is a piece of Wave Crest and, therefore, fairly valuable.

A quick look at Wilfred R. Cohen's *Wave Crest—The Glass of C.F. Monroe* reveals that this form was used for Wave Crest pieces and that this decoration was done by C.F. Monroe. This information greatly increases the value of this piece and makes it of great interest to a great number of people.

As for the damage at the top, this is what collectors call "expected damage." Jardinières were meant to hold a plant contained in another pot that was not decorative. As the plant was repeatedly put into the jardinière and subsequently removed, the top usually sustained a slight amount of damage that collectors expect to see. If the expected damage is not aesthetically unsightly, this reduces the value slightly but not significantly.

What is it worth?
At auction, this piece sold in 2005 for $1,650.

3 Two-piece box joined in the center with a metal collar. The base glass is opal, and the background is a dark fern green painted with pink flowers and white flowers. The top diameter is 4 inches and the bottom is 4½ inches. On the bottom, it is marked "Kelva Trademark."

A mark sometimes found on C.F. Monroe's "Kelva" wares.

What is it?
This is another product of the C.F. Monroe Company of Meriden, Connecticut. It was made using opal blanks just like Wave Crest, but unlike Wave Crest, which generally has a pastel coloration, "Kelva" has a dark, mottled background that resembles a design that might be found on batik. It has been speculated that this type of surface was created by daubing the color on with a sponge or a rag.

"Kelva" is very rare, and little of it was made. It is almost always decorated with flowers, and the flower seen on the piece pictured here is very typical of the embellishment on this ware. "Kelva" was made for only a few years around the turn of the twentieth century and is often—but not always—marked.

Reproductions are not a problem at the current time.

What is it worth?
$750

item 70

covered dish, milk glass "Hand and Dove"

Valued at $400

Rectangular covered dish that is 8¾ inches by 5 inches by 5 inches tall. The base has a lacy openwork edge, and the top has a depiction of a three-dimensional hand with a ring on one finger holding a dove.

what is it?

This charming Victorian box is usually referred to as the "Hand and Dove" or "Hand Holding a Bird" box, and it was made by the Atterbury Glass Company of Pittsburgh, Pennsylvania. This company traces its antecedents to 1859, when John and Thomas Atterbury joined with their brother-in-law, James Hale, to form Hale and Atterbury.

In 1862, James Reddick replaced James Hale, and the company became Atterbury and Reddick. Reddick stayed for only a short time, and in 1864, the firm became Atterbury and Company—it did not become the Atterbury Glass Company until 1893. Over the years of its existence, this company made a variety of wares, but it is most famous for its novelty covered dishes.

The most famous of these covered dishes is the ubiquitous hen on the nest, which was made in different types of glass and in a variety of sizes and styles. A number of other companies made similar hen on the nest covered boxes, and they have been reproduced widely right up to the present day.

Besides the ever popular hen on the nest, Atterbury also made covered boxes that had figural tops in the shape of such things as a rabbit, a boar's head, a reclining lion, a reclining house cat, a reclining fox, a swan, entwined fish, and a chick atop a pile of eggs—as well as the hand and dove dish pictured on page 177. In addition, Atterbury is famous for a covered dish that is entirely in the shape of a duck.

Although these dishes were widely produced in milk glass, they can be found in blue (sometimes called "blue milk glass"), green, lavender, yellow/amber, and marbleized in various shades. Sometimes, the animal boxes have eyes that are accented with inset red glass. This particular box has a ring that once was inset with a glass jewel that is now missing. In some of these (but not all), the dove also has an inset eye.

This box has been reproduced, and collectors need to be careful making purchases. Old milk glass will show "fire" around the rim when viewed through transmitted light, while the reproductions will be a rather "dead" too-white color and will generally not show the fire.

what is it worth?

Milk glass can have a surprisingly low value, but some of the figural covered dishes can command a respectable price. In this condition, the Atterbury "Hand and Dove" covered dish is worth $400. The Westmoreland reproduction of this box, from the mid-20th century, is worth $175.

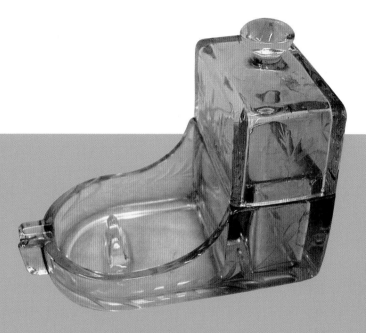

Valued at $500

4½-inch-tall covered box with attached ashtray. The entire piece is 6 inches long, and the glass is transparent yellow with wheel cut decoration. The piece is marked with an "H" inside a diamond.

what is it? Augustus H. Heisey was born in Hanover, Germany, in 1843, and immigrated to the United States the next year. The Heisey family settled in Merrittown, Pennsylvania, and Heisey began his career in the glass industry in 1861 by taking a job with the King Glass Company of Pittsburgh.

The Civil War interrupted his career in 1862 when he joined the Union Army, but he returned to his old job in 1865. Heisey left the King Glass Company to become a salesman for the Ripley Glass Company, in Pittsburgh, Pennsylvania, which was soon owned by George Duncan, who changed the name to George Duncan and Sons Glass Company.

In 1870, Heisey married Duncan's daughter, Susan, and in 1874, Duncan deeded the company to his four children. Heisey and James Duncan owned the firm by 1879. In 1893, Heisey began looking for a place to build his own glass factory, and he eventually chose Newark, Ohio, because of the availability of natural gas and cheap labor.

He opened the A.H. Heisey Glass Company there in 1896 and made very fine pressed wares, most of which were done in clear colorless glass, but there was some production in color. In late 1900, the company adopted the "H" in a diamond trademark, which had been designed by Heisey's son, George Duncan Heisey.

Augustus Heisey died in 1922, and his son E. Wilson Heisey took over. It was E. Wilson Heisey who reintroduced colored glass to Heisey. The first color was Vaseline, which went into production in 1923, and was followed by "Moon Gleam" (The company said it was the "green of moonlight on the sea.") in 1925, "Flamingo" (pink) in 1925, "Hawthorne" (amethyst) in 1927, "Marigold" in 1929, "Sahara" (yellow) in 1930, Alexandrite (shades from orchid-red to orchid-blue in transmitted light, but is greenish-blue in fluorescent light) in 1930, "Tangerine" in 1932, "Stiegel Blue" (cobalt blue) in 1933, and "Zircon" (turquoise blue-green) in 1936.

All these colors were out of production by about 1941, and today's collectors are particularly interested in colored pieces of Heisey glass. The cigarette box and ashtray shown above is in "Sahara," which was one of Heisey's most popular colors.

The box itself was designed by Rodney C. Irwin and is sometimes called the "Irwin" box, but the Heisey catalog identifies it as the number 361 ashtray and cigarette container. It was first made in 1928 and can be found in clear colorless, "Moon

Gleam," "Flamingo," "Marigold," and "Sahara." It was discontinued in 1935.

what is it worth? In this color, $500.

Related item

Typical mark associated with the products of the A.H. Heisey Company.

8½-inch-tall basket in transparent green glass. It has a rib and panel pattern and is marked with an "H" inside a diamond.

What is it?
This charming basket was made in Heisey's "Double Rib and Panel" pattern and can be found in a variety of colors including "Hawthorne" and "Moon Gleam." It is also known as Heisey's catalog number 471.

The particular example shown is in the "Moon Gleam" color, which is an adaptation and revitalization of an earlier Heisey color called "Emerald." Heisey generally spelled "Moon Gleam" as two words, but many current collectors choose to use it as one word— "Moongleam."

This color was in use at Heisey from 1925 to 1935, and the color varied over the years. Earlier pieces are deeper in color than later examples, and the piece pictured is the soft green that is associated with post-1929 "Moon Gleam."

"Moon Gleam" was a very popular color for its time and was promoted as the perfect color to be used for summertime entertaining. It was so popular that it is now the third most available of the Heisey colors after "Flamingo" and "Sahara."

What is it worth?
$250

item 72

grill plate, "Cameo"

Valued at $10

10½-inch-diameter plate with tripartite division in the center. The glass is transparent yellow, and the decoration consists of a circular center design with swags and medallion featuring a woman dancing with a scarf. There are evident mold lines and no pontil. This piece is not signed.

what is it? This is a "grill" plate, which is divided in the center to keep food separated. Plates such as this are called "grill plates" because during the early to middle years of the twentieth century, they were often used by restaurants or "grills" for food service. In addition, they were used in homes for informal meals and by those who had an aversion to various kinds of food on the same plate touching one another.

The pattern on this plate is most often called "Cameo," but it is also known as "Ballerina" or "Dancing Girl." It has been specu-lated that the "Dancing Girl" that is alluded to may be the leg-endary dancer Isadora Duncan, who died in 1927. This possibility is intriguing, but it may be fanciful. The name "Cameo" is derived from the cartouche that contains the dancing figure. This looks somewhat like a piece of Victorian cameo jewelry.

"Cameo" was made by Anchor Hocking between 1930 and 1934 and is based on a pattern called "Springtime," which was origi-nally a product of the Monongah Glass Company in Fairmont, West Virginia, which was purchased by Hocking. "Springtime"

was much more finely made than "Cameo" and is collectible in its own right.

"Cameo" was produced in green, yellow, pink, and clear colorless with a platinum rim. More "Cameo" forms were made in green than the other colors, but prices depend on both the form and the color. The progression is generally that green is the least expensive, yellow is next, and pink is the most valuable. An 11-ounce flat tumbler, for example, is about $55 in green, $100 in yellow, and $150 in pink.

Anchor Hocking made the "Cameo" grill plate in two versions. The first is like the one pictured above with a plain round rim, while the other has two closed-tab handles. Both varieties are common in yellow.

what is it worth? The "Cameo" grill plate in yellow
(both types) is $10. The green version without handles is $15, and the pink examples are $75.

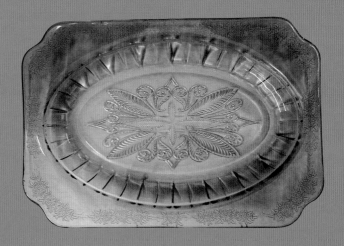

Valued at $45

Rectangular serving platter, 11¾ inches at the longest length. The design in the center is of feathers and plumes surrounding a cross made of elongated ellipses. The edge, which is notched in the corners, is surrounded with representations of small flowers and leaves arranged in a garland. The center well is separated from the rim with radial ridges, and the color is a transparent pink. There are evident mold seams and no pontil.

what is it? The Jeanette Glass Company of Jeanette, Pennsylvania, was founded in 1888 but changed its name to the Jeanette Corporation in 1970. The company went out of business in 1983.

Jeanette was responsible for many Depression glass patterns, including "Cherry Blossom," "Cubist," "Doric," "Doric and Pansy," "Floral" (also called "Poinsettia"), "Iris and Herringbone," "Sierra" (also called "Pinwheel"), "Anniversary," "Swirl," "Windsor" (alternately known as "Windsor Diamond"), and "Adam."

The piece pictured above is in the "Adam" pattern, which is one of the most popular of the Jeanette patterns. It was introduced in 1932 and was made for only a short time, until 1934. It is commonly found in pink or green, but it was also made in clear colorless, yellow, and "Delphite Blue."

"Delphite Blue" is an opaque glass that is an attractive shade of powdery blue. Jeanette also made an opaque green called "Jadite," but this color was not used to make pieces in the "Adam" pattern. "Adam" pattern Depression glass is a little more easily found in pink than it is in green, and the prices for green are only slightly higher than they are for pink. Pieces in yellow and "Delphite Blue" are appreciably higher.

Rarities in "Adam" include the lamp, the 7 1/2-inch tall vase, the butter dish that combines the "Adam" pattern with "Sierra," and the flower vase. Interestingly, the flower vase is more valuable in pink than in green. The green vase is worth about $150, while the pink example is valued at more than $650.

The only known reproduction of an "Adam" pattern piece is the butter dish. These were made in Korea in new molds that create an image that is not as distinct as that found on original items. Specifically, the veins in the feathers on the reproductions are much less distinct than they are on old pieces.

what is it worth? In pink, this platter is worth $45. In green, the value goes up just a bit, to $55.

item 74

bowl, "Manhattan"

what is it? The Anchor Hocking Glass Company of Lancaster, Ohio, was probably the largest manufacturer of the type of pressed glass that is known popularly as "Depression glass." Founded in 1880, it is still very much in business as a division of Global Home Products and claims to be the second largest supplier of glassware in the United States.

The definition of Depression glass was made over a wide time frame that far exceeds the confines of the American Great Depression of the 1930s. It was—for the most part—inexpensive pressed glassware that was primarily designed for table and kitchen use, and it came in a variety of cheerful colors.

The most popular of the colors is pink, followed by green, but examples can be found in yellow, clear colorless, ruby, amber, blue (several shades including cobalt), opalescent, iridescent marigold, and others. All of these colors are transparent, but opaque shades of green, blue, and white are also found.

Depression glass can be found in a staggering number of patterns, and Anchor Hocking was responsible for many of them, including "Bubble," "Block Optic," "Cameo," "Lace Edge," "Miss America," "Mayfair," "Princess," "Sandwich" (an interpretation of Boston and Sandwich's "lacy" glass), and the one pictured above, "Manhattan."

"Manhattan" was made between 1938 and 1943, and it is most commonly found in clear colorless, but pink, green, ruby, and

Valued at $35

Bowl, 9-inch diameter, clear colorless glass. The body has heavy ribbed ridges running horizontally and ribbed tab handles. There are mold seams evident, and there is no pontil.

iridized examples can be found on occasion. Of the colors other than clear colorless, pink is the one that shows up the most, but the price differential between clear colorless and pink can be startling. A 10$\frac{1}{4}$-inch-diameter "Manhattan" dinner plate, for example, is $30 in clear colorless, but in pink that same plate is valued at approximately $250. An even wider disparity exists with the coffee cup and saucer, which in clear colorless is a mere $20, but in pink the price soars to around $300.

It should be understood, however, that this great disparity in price between clear colorless and pink is not always the case. The price for an open sugar bowl in clear colorless, for example, is $15, but in pink, the price rises to only $18. Similar small differences also occur for the handled berry bowl, the 9$\frac{1}{2}$-inch fruit bowl, the compote, the creamer, the relish tray with inserts, and the tumbler.

Collectors need to be aware that Anchor Hocking introduced a new line called "Park Avenue" in 1987 that is very similar to "Manhattan." The best way to tell the difference is that "Park Avenue" sizes and shapes are a bit different from the original "Manhattan," and "Park Avenue" was made in blue, but "Manhattan" never was.

"Manhattan" is very popular with collectors who like its sleek lines and pre–World War II modern feel.

what is it worth? $35

item 75

oblong dish, Fostoria "Heather"

Valued at $50

11⅛-by-7-inch oblong dish with a slightly pinched waist giving the hint of a figure "8" shape. Two handles, with three slanted divisions. The glass is clear colorless, and the piece is decorated with etched representations of flowers and leaves. It is unsigned.

what is it?

This three-part relish dish was made by the Fostoria Glass Company of Moundsville, West Virginia. This company was founded in Fostoria, Ohio, in 1887 but moved to Moundsville in 1891. It was an important producer of pressed glass and lamps, and in 1915, introduced the famous raised-cube design called "American," which was made until the company closed in 1986.

In the 1920s, Fostoria began introducing elegant tableware in colors such as canary, amber, blue, orchid, green, and black. By the late 1930s, the company was recognized as the largest manufacturer of handmade glassware in the world, and during the course of their history, produced more than 1,150 patterns of glass. Today, this company is most famous for its stemware production made during the third and early fourth quarter of the twentieth century.

The piece pictured is in Fostoria's "Century" shape, which was first made in 1945 and continued in production until 1985. It is its number 2630 pattern, and the hardest pieces to find are the three-pint ice-lipped pitcher, the 8 1/2-inch-tall oval vase, and the condiment set. This particular example is decorated with Fostoria's number 6037 etched pattern called "Heather."

"Heather" was reportedly made from 1949 to 1971 and can be found on a wide variety of tableware items that range from water goblets and dinner plates to candlesticks and mayonnaise bowls.

what is it worth?

This three-part relish is valued at $50. Values of other "Heather" pieces include the cruet, $145; the tall water goblet, $35; the low water goblet, $30; the dinner plate, $85 (with no significant scratches); the three-pint ice-lipped jug, $265; and the mayonnaise set (bowl, under plate, and ladle), $70.

item 76

"Fire-King" range set

Valued at $150

Five white glass containers, one with a glass lid and four with metal shaker tops. All are decorated in red and black with stylized images of a potted plant. The pieces have evident mold lines and are unsigned.

what is it? In 1940, the Anchor Hocking Company of Lancaster, Ohio, introduced a line of heat-resistant "oven proof" glassware that it called "Fire-King." "Fire-King" came in a variety of colors, including clear colorless, jade green ("Jade-ite"), sapphire blue (a transparent light blue), and many others.

Anchor Hocking called the pieces that were in milk white or beige glass "Vitrock," and this is the glass used to make the set pictured. From the late 1940s through much of the 1960s, it was fashionable for kitchens to have a range set that was designed to sit on the back of the stove.

These sets usually consisted of a grease or "drippings" jar (the large covered piece shown on the previous page) and shakers that most commonly held salt, pepper, flour, and sugar. On some occasions, these range sets might also include spice shakers—but these are considered to be rather unusual and rare.

Grease jars were very handy devices because if the cook needed to drain the grease from the breakfast bacon, all he or she had to do was pour it into the "drippings" jar without moving from the stove. Or if a sauce needed thickening, the flower shaker was right there—and if something needed a bit of sugar, the shaker was at hand.

This "Fire-King Vitrock" range set has all its components and the original lids. Recently, it has been reported that the lids have value by themselves, and collectors are willing to pay almost as much for the old lids in excellent condition as they are for the complete set of jar and lid.

These "Fire-King Vitrock" sets came with several distinct patterns. They were "Circles with Flowers," "Circles," "Flower Pots," and "Red Tulips." The first three of these can be found in several color schemes, for example, "Circles with Flowers" was made in blue, red, or black.

The particular pattern on this range set is "Red Flower Pots." It also came in a green version that is somewhat harder to find and a bit more valuable.

what is it worth? $150 for the complete set.

item 77

vase, Pilgrim

Valued at $1,800

9½-inch-tall vase, bulbous body to flared lip. The piece is composed of five layers of glass, with the base being frosted clear with green, pink, red, and white on top. The decoration is a profusion of flowers and leaves with winged fairies hidden among the blossoms. The piece has a polished bottom and is signed "954031 D/P 1997 Kelsey Pilgrim." It is in perfect condition.

what is it? In 1949, engineer Alfred Knobler bought the Tri State Glass Manufacturing Company in Huntington, West Virginia, and began making glass. Seven years later, he moved the company to a new facility in Ceredo, West Virginia, just a few miles from Huntington.

The firm was called the Pilgrim Glass Company, and over the years it made a wide variety of glass that ranged from crackle glass to its most famous product, cranberry glass. It also made glass animals in the Venetian style, and in 1992, after buying the molds from the old Phoenix Glass Company and the Consolidated Lamp and

Glass Company, it began making reissues of many of the pieces manufactured by these two related companies (all of the new production is clearly marked "Pilgrim Glass" on the bottom).

Perhaps Pilgrim's most outstanding product, and the one that will secure its position in the hearts of collectors, is the cameo glass line, which was started in the late 1980s by art director Kelsey

Murphy. This cameo glass line was not made in the classic sense by carving away layers of differently colored glass to reveal a design but was made by sandblasting away the differently colored layers.

At the time this project began, it was said that it was impossible to make a cameo piece with five layers of color, but Murphy and her associates managed to make pieces with as many as fourteen. The range of Pilgrim's cameo glass is truly extraordinary, and collectors can find everything from Christmas ornaments to large plaques decorated with elaborate scenic designs.

Decorations include depictions of animals, flowers, landscapes, Christmas themed items, and athletes such as swimmers, among others. Unfortunately, production stopped at Pilgrim in 2001, and the company closed in March 2002.

Although this glass is relatively recent, collector interest is high, with many feeling that this glass will be very important in the future. It should be mentioned, however, that there are some Pilgrim cameo-like pieces that are very simple and usually made with only two colors—red or blue on a frosted background. The designs are generally representations of leaves or flowers done with little detail. These lesser cameo pieces were made in relatively large quantities and sold in department stores. Their monetary worth is much less than the value of the more elaborate and artistically done Pilgrim cameo pieces.

what is it worth? This piece is a developmental proof (indicated by the D/P in the signature), which means it was not a production piece. The "1997" in the signature indicates the date of manufacture. It is worth $1,800.

Glossary

Acid cut back
This technique required a glass vessel to be "cased," which means it has two or more layers of differently colored glass on top of one another. In one method, a design is inked onto the outer surface and then all of the other areas are coated with a protective wax that is impervious to acid. The piece is immersed in acid, and the inked areas are cut away to the color layer below, while the areas coated in wax are left unaffected. This leaves a two-color design with one color slightly raised above the other that resembles cameo glass without the maker having to do all of the laborious hand cutting away of the various layers of glass. A number of important American glass makers used this technique, including Tiffany, Steuben, and Mt. Washington.

Air trap
In this process, a gather of glass is blown into a mold that leaves a pattern of indentations on the outer surface. Next, the glass is encased in another layer of glass that traps air in the indentations that were left in the first step. These indentations are usually arranged in a variety of patterns that include diamond, circle, herringbone, or teardrop shapes. The finished product has a shimmering almost underwater appearance.

Alkali
This is a soluble salt such as soda or potash that serves as a flux and allows the silica ("sand") used in making glass to fuse at a lower temperature. The alkali makes up as much as 20 percent of the ingredients in a glass batch.

Annealing
The process of cooling glass uniformly after it is made. Some parts of a glass object cool more quickly than other parts, and this causes stress that can lead to cracks and serious damage. To prevent this, glass pieces are put in an annealing oven or "Lehr" after they are made and allowed to cool down gradually at consistent temperatures that diminish over time.

Blown or free-blown glass
This is the process of shaping a mass of molten glass (called a "parison" or a "gather") by blowing or "huffing" air through a

hollow blow pipe. This produces a bubble in the center of the hot glass that is expanded by more blowing until it reaches the desired size. In addition, while the air is being blown into the molten glass, the mass is being shaped by tools to get it into the desired form. Blown or "free-blown" glass can be distinguished (in most cases) by the lack of mold lines and the presence of a flat bottom that has been ground down or a pontil that is the size and shape of a coin that ranges from dime to silver-dollar size (or in rare instances even larger). An exception to this is when glass is blown into a snap case, which will leave no pontil mark.

Blown in mold

This is the process of blowing molten glass into a mold that has a pattern on the inside. The pattern, be it raised or recessed, is imparted to the surface of the glass, which assumes the shape and design of the interior of the mold. On a piece that has been blown in mold, the pattern can be felt on the inside as well as the outside.

Cased glass

Glassware made with two or more layers of different colors is said to be "cased." The process begins by blowing a gather of glass and opening up one end and placing the glass into a mold. Next, another gather of glass in a different color is blown into the first gather, and this process can be repeated for as many times as desired, but five times would be considered a high number. After the layers are blown, the glass is heated so that the various layers will fuse together. The layers in cased glass are substantial and relatively thick as opposed to the layers in glass that has been "flashed," which involves dipping glass of one color into molten glass of another. This produces a fairly thin coating that can be damaged in use. Cased glass is often used to make cameo or acid cut back glass in which designs are cut through the layers of differently colored glass to create a pictorial or geometric design. Cased glass has been made since Roman times.

Crystal

Classically, the term "crystal" refers to rock crystal, which is a kind of clear quartz that was often carved into vessels or made into pendant decorations for lighting fixtures. The term, however, has come to include any high-quality, transparent, colorless glass that resembles rock crystal. In modern usage, crystal is usually a glass made using a high lead content of at least 24 percent, which is called "half-lead" crystal in the trade. Glass made with

30 percent lead is referred to as "full-lead" crystal or "cristal superieur."

Cut glass

A method of decorating glass that has been in use since the eighth century. In the process, the surface of the glass is embellished with facets, miter cuts, grooves, pictorial images, and/or panels that are cut into the piece using a rotating stone or iron wheel. There were three main periods of American cut glass. The first was from approximately 1770 to 1830 and is distinguished by engravings of swags, birds, flowers, or stars done in the English manner. These appear alone or in conjunction with simple flute cuts, shaped diamond cuts, pillar cuts, or the English strawberry diamond and fan design. The second cut glass period is called the "Middle Period" and lasted from 1830 to around the time of the American centennial celebration in 1876. During this period, the first colored cut glass appeared, and the best pieces were decorated with intricately engraved patterns that could be very sophisticated. Most "Middle Period" American cut glass, however, was cut with broad panels of flute cuts. The third period is known as the "American Brilliant Period" and lasted from around 1880 to about 1910. This is the time frame in which cut glass became very popular with the public and was an important gift item for brides and wives on their anniversaries and birthdays. American Brilliant Period cut glass is distinguished by thick, heavy, high-quality, hand-blown, lead glass that was intricately and deeply cut with geometric patterns such as hobstars, fans, notched prisms, and cane (also called "chair bottom") designs. This latter type of cut glass is most often found in clear colorless glass. Very rarely, however, it can be found in colored glass or colored glass that has been cut through to reveal a clear colorless layer below (called "color cut to clear"). It is very prismatic in nature, and the cuts can be sharp—although not as sharp as the modern reproductions that are cut using laser technology.

Ductile

The physical property of being able to be drawn out or molded into a desired shape. Molten glass is very ductile.

Engraving

The process of decorating the surface of glassware using a variety of instruments, including a diamond point, metal needle, or a rotating wheel. This type of decoration usually requires the glass vessel being used to have walls that are relatively thick to withstand the pressures of the engraving tools.

Etching

In this process, hydrofluoric acid is used to cut away the surface of a piece of glass and leave behind a predetermined decoration. The first step in this method involves covering the surface of the glass with a substance that will resist the operation of the acid. Then a design is cut or scratched through with a sharp tool and the vessel is immersed in the acid. The acid will eat away at the cut or scratched areas, leaving a frosted indentation, but the rest of the surface will be untouched. Etching can be done on glass with relatively thin walls.

Flashing

This is the process of superimposing a thin layer of glass onto a much thicker layer, generally by dipping the thicker layer in molten glass of a different color.

Flint glass

This term is really a misnomer. There was a time in England when calcined or ground flint (a type of finely grained quartz) was substituted for other materials as a source for the silica used in making glass. At about the same time this was being done, lead was being introduced to increase the brilliance of the glass, and the lead glass became labeled with the flint name. Therefore, "flint" glass is really glass made with lead.

Gather

A blob of molten glass that is "gathered" from the glass furnace on the end of a blow pipe or gathering rod in preparation to blow a glass vessel.

Knop

A component of the stem of a drinking glass or other glass vessel that is usually spherical or oblate. They come in many styles and can be hollow or solid. There may be a single knop on a stem, or there may be multiples. When more than one knop is used on a stem, they may be the same size and shape or they may vary. In some cases, the knop is the "swelling" where the stem joins with the bowl of the vessel, the foot, or both. Knops are also used in the middle of stems to give them shape. Some of the shapes of knops are acorns, balls, buttons, cones, dumbbells, eggs, melons, and mushrooms.

Marver

A table made from iron, wood, or marble on which molten glass is rolled after it is taken from the furnace attached to the blow pipe. Sometimes, shards of glass are sprinkled on the surface of the marver and when the molten glass is rolled over these pieces, they adhere, giving the object a textured surface unless the parison is then reheated and expanded further. In this case, the shards of glass will be incorporated into the body and the surface will be smooth.

Molding

From a very early time, molds were made to assist in the formation of glass vessels. Initially they were designed to have glass blown into them, but later, they were used by pushing glass into them with a plunger to make "pressed" glass. Molds were used for several purposes—one was to impart a design to the outer surface, and another was to form the entire vessel. Molds were made from a variety of materials including clay, wood, carved stone, and, later, metal. One-part molds were used early on, but two-part hinged molds came along later and were followed by more complicated three- and four-part molds.

Opal glass

A translucent white glass that is made partially opaque by adding tin oxide. In transmitted light, it often shows reddish or brownish tones. It should not be confused with milk glass, which is similar in appearance but is much more opaque.

Opaque

The quality of not transmitting light. Most glass that is called "opaque" is in fact at least slightly translucent and will allow some light to pass through. Generally, if it cannot be seen through and if it transmits very little light, a piece of glass is said to be "opaque."

Parison or paraison

There are two main definitions of this term. The one in favor today is of a gather of glass on a blow pipe that has had a bubble blown into it. Previously, this was defined as a rounded mass of molten glass that has been gathered from the furnace and rolled on a marver.

Pontil

This is the mark or "scar" found on the base of glass pieces that have been free-blown. The process of blowing starts with a gather of glass from the furnace that is shaped by puffing air in the mass until a bubble of a desired size is formed. At this point, an iron rod called a "punty" is attached to the glass mass opposite the blow pipe. The pipe is then broken off, and the punty is used as a sort of handle to support the glass while the mouth is being opened, handles are attached (if necessary), and the final forming is completed. When the piece is finished, the pontil rod is removed, which leaves a roughly circular area of jagged glass on what would be the object's bottom side or base. Sometimes the punty is pushed up into the glass to form a conical depression that keeps the jagged pontil scar from touching a surface or making the vessel unsteady. This conical depression is sometimes called a "kick-up," especially when it is quite deep. When the bottom is left flat, the jagged glass is ground down, leaving a slightly depressed polished area that is roughly circular and can range in size from that of a dime to a silver dollar or even larger. On occasion, the entire bottom is ground down, leaving an entirely flat surface with no circular pontil depression.

Pressed glass

This type of glassware is made by "injecting" a blow of molten glass into a mold using a plunger. This is a cheap, quick method of mass producing a glass vessel with some sort of pattern. Pressed glass made its first appearance in the United States in 1827 and in Europe just a few years earlier. Unlike glass that has been blown in a mold, pressed glass has a very smooth interior. Pressed glass can be found in a huge variety of patterns that range from simple geometrics to elaborate pictorial designs. In the late nineteenth century, much pressed glass was made to imitate more expensive cut glass. Pressed glass can be easily differentiated from cut glass because the designs on pressed glass are smooth and rounded while the designs on cut glass tend to be much sharper. Also, pre-1910 cut glass has no mold lines, while pressed glass pieces do.

Prunt

A blob of glass affixed to the surface of a piece of glass as a decorative element or when used on a drinking glass as a means of providing a safer grip for the drinker. Prunts were sometimes given the form of a lion's head mask or perhaps of a raspberry.

Rigoree or rigaree

A decoration on blown glass consisting of a narrow, raised ribbon or parallel ribbons of glass placed by hand on the outer surface of a glass vessel. These ribbons generally have ladderlike tool marks running the length or are laid down in an almost wavelike fashion.

Translucent

The quality of permitting the transmission of light through an object but with enough diffusion that nothing can be clearly seen.

Transparent

The quality of permitting the transmission of light through an object without diffusion so that objects can be clearly seen.

Wafer

Before and during the early nineteenth century, glass pieces were often made in several parts and the components were put together using a small, thin piece of glass that collectors call a "wafer."

Photo Credits

Item 1: Stiegel bottle
Item courtesy of Green Valley Auctions, Inc., Virginia
Photo by William H. McGuffin

Item 2: sunburst flask
Item courtesy of Green Valley Auctions, Inc., Virginia
Photo by William H. McGuffin

Item 3: Washington and Jackson flask
Item courtesy of Green Valley Auctions, Inc., Virginia
Photo by William H. McGuffin

Item 4: Pittsburgh sugar bowl
Item courtesy of Green Valley Auctions, Inc., Virginia
Photo by William H. McGuffin

Item 5: witch ball
Item courtesy of Green Valley Auctions, Inc., Virginia
Photo by William H. McGuffin

Related item: bowl with spherical cover
Item courtesy of Green Valley Auctions, Inc., Virginia
Photo by William H. McGuffin

Item 6: "Lily-pad" jug
Item courtesy of Green Valley Auctions, Inc., Virginia
Photo by William H. McGuffin

Item 7: money box
Item courtesy of Northeast Auctions, Portsmouth, New
Hampshire

Item 8: syrup pitcher, Rubina
Item courtesy of the Houston Museum, Chattanooga, Tennessee
Photo by Richard H. Crane

Item 9: vase, Amberina
Item courtesy of Richard H. Crane
Photo by Richard H. Crane

Item 10: pitcher, plated Amberina
Item courtesy of the Houston Museum, Chattanooga, Tennessee
Photo by Richard H. Crane

Item 11: vase in stand, Wheeling Peach Blow
Item courtesy of the Houston Museum, Chattanooga, Tennessee
Photo by Richard H. Crane

Related item: Wheeling Peach Blow pitcher
Item courtesy of the Houston Museum, Chattanooga, Tennessee
Photo by Richard H. Crane

Item 12: pitcher, New England Peach Blow
Item courtesy of the Houston Museum, Chattanooga, Tennessee
Photo by Richard H. Crane

Related item: "Agata" tumbler
Item courtesy of Green Valley Auctions, Inc., Virginia
Photo by William H. McGuffin

Item 13: tumbler, "Green Opaque"
Item courtesy of Green Valley Auctions, Inc., Virginia
Photo by William H. McGuffin

Item 14: pitcher, Mt. Washington Peach Blow
Item courtesy of the Houston Museum, Chattanooga, Tennessee
Photo by Richard H. Crane

Item 15: biscuit jar, "Royal Flemish"
Item courtesy of Green Valley Auctions, Inc., Virginia
Photo by William H. McGuffin

Item 16: cruet, Burmese
Item courtesy of the Houston Museum, Chattanooga, Tennessee
Photo by Richard H. Crane

Item 17: vase, "Napoli"
Item courtesy of Green Valley Auctions, Inc., Virginia
Photo by William H. McGuffin

Item 18 bowl, "Crown Milano"
Item courtesy of Green Valley Auctions, Inc., Virginia
Photo by William H. McGuffin

Item 19: pitcher, "Overshot"
Item courtesy of the Houston Museum, Chattanooga, Tennessee
Photo by Richard H. Crane

Item 20: bowl, Mt. Washington cameo
Item courtesy of Green Valley Auctions, Inc., Virginia
Photo by William H. McGuffin

Item 21: pitcher, "Pomona"
Item courtesy of the Houston Museum, Chattanooga, Tennessee
Photo by Richard H. Crane

Related item: "Pomona" tumble-up
Item courtesy of Green Valley Auctions, Inc., Virginia
Photo by William H. McGuffin

Item 22: vase, "Mary Gregory"
Item courtesy of the Houston Museum, Chattanooga, Tennessee
Photo by Richard H. Crane

Item 23: vase, "Mother-of-Pearl Satin Glass"
Item courtesy of the Houston Museum, Chattanooga, Tennessee
Photo by Richard H. Crane

Related item: "Mother-of-Pearl Satin Glass" pitcher
Item courtesy of the Houston Museum, Chattanooga, Tennessee
Photo by Richard H. Crane

Related item "Mother-of-Pearl Satin Glass" pitcher
Item courtesy of the Houston Museum, Chattanooga, Tennessee
Photo by Richard H. Crane

Item 24: ewer, "Rainbow Mother-of-Pearl"
Item courtesy of the Houston Museum, Chattanooga, Tennessee
Photo by Richard H. Crane

Item 25: pitcher, Tiffany
Item courtesy of the Houston Museum, Chattanooga, Tennessee
Photo by Richard H. Crane

Related item: Tiffany vase
Item courtesy of Green Valley Auctions, Inc., Virginia
Photo by William H. McGuffin

Item 26: vase, Tiffany flower form
Item courtesy of the Houston Museum, Chattanooga, Tennessee
Photo by Richard H. Crane

Related item: Tiffany vase
Item courtesy of Green Valley Auctions, Inc., Virginia
Photo by William H. McGuffin

Item 27: bowl, Tiffany
Item courtesy of Green Valley Auctions, Inc., Virginia
Photo by William H. McGuffin

Item 28: vase, Steuben "Aurene"
Item courtesy of the Houston Museum, Chattanooga, Tennessee
Photo by Richard H. Crane

Related item: Steuben blue "Aurene" bowl
Item courtesy of the Houston Museum, Chattanooga, Tennessee
Photo by Richard H. Crane

Item 29: goblets, Steuben
Item courtesy of Richard H. Crane
Photo by Richard H. Crane

Item 30: vase, Steuben acid cut back
Item courtesy of the Houston Museum, Chattanooga, Tennessee
Photo by Richard H. Crane

Item 31: vase, Steuben
Item courtesy of Green Valley Auctions, Inc., Virginia
Photo by William H. McGuffin

Item 32: vase, Durand
Item courtesy of the Houston Museum, Chattanooga, Tennessee
Photo by Richard H. Crane

Related item: Durand vase
Item courtesy of Green Valley Auctions, Inc., Virginia
Photo by William H. McGuffin

Item 33: pitcher, Fenton
Item courtesy of the Houston Museum, Chattanooga, Tennessee
Photo by Richard H. Crane

Related item: opalescent syrup pitcher
Item courtesy of the Houston Museum, Chattanooga, Tennessee
Photo by Richard H. Crane

Related item: opalescent pitcher "Stars and Stripes"
Item courtesy of Green Valley Auctions, Inc., Virginia
Photo by William H. McGuffin

Item 34: pitcher, "Middle Period" cut glass
Item courtesy of Green Valley Auctions, Inc., Virginia
Photo by William H. McGuffin

Item 35: water pitcher, red cut to clear
Item courtesy of the Houston Museum, Chattanooga, Tennessee
Photo by Richard H. Crane

Item 36: bowl, American Brilliant Period cut glass
Item courtesy of Green Valley Auctions, Inc., Virginia
Photo by William H. McGuffin

Item 37: carafe, American Brilliant Period cut glass
Item courtesy of Green Valley Auctions, Inc., Virginia
Photo by William H. McGuffin

Item 38: oval tray, Sinclaire cut glass
Item courtesy of Green Valley Auctions, Inc., Virginia
Photo by William H. McGuffin

Item 39: Pitcher with silver top, green cut to clear, intaglio
Item courtesy of Green Valley Auctions, Inc., Virginia
Photo by William H. McGuffin

Related item: intaglio cut vase
Item courtesy of Green Valley Auctions, Inc., Virginia
Photo by William H. McGuffin

Item 40: paperweight, Boston and Sandwich Glass Company
Item courtesy of the Houston Museum, Chattanooga, Tennessee
Photo by Richard H. Crane

Item 41: salt, "Basket of Flowers"
Item courtesy of Green Valley Auctions, Inc., Virginia
Photo by William H. McGuffin

Item 42: salt, "Lafayet"
Item courtesy of Green Valley Auctions, Inc., Virginia
Photo by William H. McGuffin

Item 43: cup plate, "Chancellor Livingston"
Item courtesy of Green Valley Auctions, Inc., Virginia
Photo by William H, McGuffin

Related item: cup plate, "Lee/Rose #227"
Item courtesy of Green Valley Auctions, Inc., Virginia
Photo by William H. McGuffin

Item 44: compote, "Princess Feather Medallion and Basket of Flowers"
Item courtesy of Green Valley Auctions, Inc., Virginia
Photo by William H. McGuffin

Item 45: windowpane, lacy
Item courtesy of Green Valley Auctions, Inc., Virginia
Photo by William H. McGuffin

Item 46: Vase, "Tulip"
Item courtesy of Green Valley Auctions, Inc., Virginia
Photo by William H. McGuffin

Item 47: compote, open work
Item courtesy of Green Valley Auctions, Inc., Virginia
Photo by William H. McGuffin

Item 48: lamp base, cut overlay
Item courtesy of Green Valley Auctions, Inc., Virginia
Photo by William H. McGuffin

Item 49: cream pitcher, "Ashburton"
Item courtesy of Green Valley Auctions, Inc., Virginia
Photo by William H. McGuffin

Item 50: compote, "Ribbed Palm"
Item courtesy of Green Valley Auctions, Inc., Virginia
Photo by William H. McGuffin

Item 51: compote, "Horn of Plenty"
Item courtesy of Green Valley Auctions, Inc., Virginia
Photo by William H. McGuffin

Related item: "Horn of Plenty" with Washington head
Item courtesy of Green Valley Auctions, Inc., Virginia
Photo by William H. McGuffin

Item 52: compote, "Three Face"
Item courtesy of Green Valley Auctions, Inc., Virginia
Photo by William H. McGuffin

Item 53: Oval compote, "Jumbo"
Item courtesy of Green Valley Auctions, Inc., Virginia
Photo by William H. McGuffin

Related item: "Jumbo" castor set
Item courtesy of Green Valley Auctions, Inc., Virginia
Photo by William H. McGuffin

Item 54: butter dish, custard glass, "Louis XV"
Item courtesy of the Houston Museum, Chattanooga, Tennessee
Photo by Richard H. Crane

Related item: custard glass cruet, "Argonaut Shell"
Item courtesy of the Houston Museum, Chattanooga, Tennessee
Photo by Richard H. Crane

Item 55: pitcher, chocolate glass, "Cactus"
Item courtesy of the Houston Museum, Chattanooga, Tennessee
Photo by Richard H. Crane

Related item: chocolate glass mug, "Outdoor Drinking Scene"
Item courtesy of the Houston Museum, Chattanooga, Tennessee
Photo by Richard H. Crane

Item 56: butter dish, "Holly Amber"
Item courtesy of the Houston Museum, Chattanooga, Tennessee
Photo by Richard H. Crane

Related item: "Holly Amber" tumbler
Item courtesy of Green Valley Auctions, Inc., Virginia
Photo by William H. McGuffin

Item 57: spooner, "Single Vine Bellflower"
Item courtesy of Green Valley Auctions, Inc., Virginia
Photo by William H. McGuffin

Item 58: table setting, "Monkey"
Item courtesy of Green Valley Auctions, Inc., Virginia
Photo by William H. McGuffin

Item 59: sugar bowl, "Log Cabin"
Item courtesy of Green Valley Auctions, Inc., Virginia
Photo by William H. McGuffin

Item 60: water pitcher, "Memphis"
Item courtesy of the Houston Museum, Chattanooga, Tennessee
Photo by Richard H. Crane

Related item: "Klondike" cream pitcher
Item courtesy of the Houston Museum, Chattanooga, Tennessee
Photo by Richard H. Crane

Item 61: water pitcher, "Cabbage Leaf"
Item courtesy of the Houston Museum, Chattanooga, Tennessee
Photo by Richard H. Crane

Item 62: celery vase, "Actress"
Item courtesy of Richard H. Crane
Photo by Richard H. Crane

Item 63: water pitcher, "Wading Heron"
Item courtesy of the Houston Museum, Chattanooga, Tennessee
Photo by Richard H. Crane

Item 64: water pitcher, "Old Oaken Bucket"
Item courtesy of the Houston Museum, Chattanooga, Tennessee
Photo by Richard H. Crane

Item 65: carnival glass bowl, "Dugan Cherry"
Item courtesy of Richard H. Crane
Photo by Richard H. Crane

Item 66: carnival glass bowls, "Peacock and Urn"
Item courtesy of Green Valley Auctions, Inc., Virginia
Photo by William H. McGuffin

Related item: "Good Luck" bowl
Item courtesy of Green Valley Auctions, Inc., Virginia
Photo by William H. McGuffin

Related item: "Dahlia" tumbler
Item courtesy of Green Valley Auctions, Inc., Virginia
Photo by William H. McGuffin

Related item: "Butterfly and Tulip" bowl
Item courtesy of Green Valley Auctions, Inc., Virginia
Photo by William H. McGuffin

Item 67: carnival glass bowl, "Dragon and Lotus"
Item courtesy of Green Valley Auctions, Inc., Virginia
Photo by William H. McGuffin

Item 68: carnival glass bowl, "Big Fish"
Item courtesy of Green Valley Auctions, Inc., Virginia
Photo by William H. McGuffin

Item 69: box, "Wave Crest"
Item courtesy of the Houston Museum, Chattanooga, Tennessee
Photo by Richard H. Crane

Related item: "Kelva box"
Item courtesy of the Houston Museum, Chattanooga, Tennessee
Photo by Richard H. Crane

Related item: "Wave Crest" jardinière
Item courtesy of Green Valley Auctions, Inc., Virginia
Photo by William H. McGuffin

Item courtesy of Green Valley Auctions, Inc., Virginia
Photo by William H. McGuffin

Item 70: covered dish, milk glass, "Hand and Dove"
Item courtesy of the Houston Museum, Chattanooga, Tennessee
Photo by Richard H. Crane

Item 71: box and attached ashtray, Heisey
Item courtesy of Kingston Pike Antiques Mall, Knoxville,
Tennessee
Photo by Richard H. Crane

Item courtesy of Kingston Pike Antiques Mall, Knoxville,
Tennessee
Photo by Richard H. Crane

Item 72: grill plate, "Cameo"
Item courtesy of Kingston Pike Antiques Mall, Knoxville,
Tennessee
Photo by Richard H. Crane

Item 73: platter, "Adam"
Item courtesy of Kingston Pike Antiques Mall, Knoxville,
Tennessee
Photo by Richard H. Crane

Item 74: bowl, "Manhattan"
Item courtesy of Kingston Pike Antiques Mall, Knoxville,
Tennessee
Photo by Richard H. Crane

Item 75: oblong dish, Fostoria "Heather"
Item courtesy of Kingston Pike Antiques Mall, Knoxville,
Tennessee
Photo by Richard H. Crane

Item 76: "Fire-King" range set
Item courtesy of Elaine Tomber Tindell
Photo by Richard H. Crane

Item 77: vase, Pilgrim
Item courtesy of Richard H. Crane
Photo by Richard H. Crane

Index